The Israeli Economy

The Israeli Economy

Paul Rivlin

Westview Press
BOULDER • SAN FRANCISCO • OXFORD

This Westview softcover edition is printed on acid-free paper and bound in library-quality, coated covers that carry the highest rating of the National Association of State Textbook Administrators, in consultation with the Association of American Publishers and the Book Manufacturers' Institute.

Published in 1992 in the United States of America by Westview Press, Inc., 5500 Central Avenue, Boulder, Colorado 80301-2847, and in the United Kingdom by Westview Press, 36 Lonsdale Road, Summertown, Oxford OX2 7EW

Library of Congress Cataloging-in-Publication Data
Rivlin, Paul.
The Israeli economy / Paul Rivlin.
p. cm.
Includes bibliographical references and index.
ISBN 0-8133-7653-X
1. Israel—Economic conditions. I. Title.
HC415.25.R58 1992
330.95694—dc20 91-38465
CIP

Printed and bound in the United States of America

The paper used in this publication meets the requirements of the American National Standard for Permanence of Paper for Printed Library Materials Z39.48-1984.

10 9 8 7 6 5 4 3 2 1

To Rosemary, Ben, and Alexander

Contents

Tables and Figures

Tables

Figures

Preface

Twelve years ago when I taught a graduate course on the economic development of the Middle East at London University, I was surprised that there was no up-to-date book in English on the Israeli economy. The most recently published general book, suitable for students, was Nadav Halevi and Ruth Klinov-Malul's *The Economic Development of Israel*, published in 1968. Since then Yoram Ben Porat has edited a collection of papers on the economy in a volume entitled *The Israeli Economy: Maturing Through Crises*, published in 1985. This work deals with many of the major problems facing the economy in the period leading up to the economic stabilization program of 1985.

I therefore decided to write a nontechnical, general guide to the economy covering the period since 1985. As I studied the issues in greater detail, particularly the political economy of Israel, I became more critical of the performance of the economy and the way in which it has been managed. I have as a result included a discussion of economic reform and the context in which it might occur. Although this book is aimed at a non-Israeli readership, it does not attempt to hide the problems that have arisen in the economy because of domestic constraints as well as difficult external conditions.

In writing this book I have benefitted from many discussions with friends and colleagues. I would like, in this connection, to thank Yair Aharoni, Daniel Gottlieb, Nahum Gross, Jonathan Katz, Yaacov Kop, Azriel Levi, Amnon Neubach, Yoram Peri, Francis Wood, and Ben Ami Zuckerman for their suggestions and comments. Adam Klug read and commented on several chapters of the draft and provided me with many insights about the economy. Tami Bercovitz, Barbara Davison, Michael Josephs, and Zena Rivlin proofread parts of the draft; Rutti Dagan and Diana Rubanenko assisted in word processing. Thanks to Jacques Gansler for his insights into the functioning of defense markets. I am also grateful to Barbara Ellington of Westview Press for her encouragement.

Finally, my thanks to Rosemary for her help, encouragement, and patience. Without her this book could not have been written.

I am, of course, solely responsible for any errors and omissions.

Paul Rivlin

Notes on the Text

Extensive use has been made of the publications of the Central Bureau of Statistics of the government of Israel and of the Bank of Israel. Major references have been indicated in the text.

The Israeli lira, or pound, was replaced by the shekel in 1980 at a rate of 10 lirot to 1 shekel. The shekel was replaced by the new shekel in 1986 at a rate of 1,000 shekels to 1 new shekel.

Abbreviations used in the text include the following:

bn.	billions (thousands of millions)
m.	millions
fob	free on board
cif	cost, insurance, and freight

Due to rounding, some columns in the tables do not sum to the totals given.

Unless otherwise stated, figures are in current prices and those in U.S. dollars are converted at current exchange rates. The annual average exchange rates of the new shekel against the U.S. dollar were as follows:

1985	1.1789
1986	1.4878
1987	1.5947
1988	1.5989
1989	1.9164
1990	2.0162

1

The Economic Development of Israel: 1948–1985

The purpose of this book is to analyze the performance and institutions of the Israeli economy. This analysis will be done using macroeconomic, sectoral, and historical methods.

As Israel experiences the largest wave of immigration in forty years, the central problem facing the economy is lack of growth. Since 1973 the economy has stagnated; the causes and effects of this stagnation are at the center of this study. Without economic growth new immigrants and many of the unemployed among the veteran population will face a continuing lack of work opportunities.

Between 1950 and 1973 Israel's gross national product (GNP) grew at an average annual rate of about 9 percent, one of the highest rates in the world (see Figure 1.1).[1] Since 1973, however, it has experienced slow growth that has at times barely exceeded that of the rate of population increase (see Table 1.1). It has been plagued by balance-of-payments problems, and between 1979 and 1985 prices rose by over 100 percent a year. Despite large government expenditure and budget deficits, the provision of public goods such as education has declined to unsatisfactory levels. At the same time tax levels are among the highest in the world, with severe negative effects on incentives to work and invest. These problems, which are sectoral and political, are due in part to the confrontation between Israel and much of the Arab world.

There were a number of distinct phases in the development of the economy, marked by changes in growth rates and economic policy. It is necessary to go back as far as the immediate prestate period in order to trace the origins of economic policy.

1939–1945: The Effects of the Second World War

The 1939–1945 period was one of relative prosperity, mainly because the economy of the Yishuv (the Jewish community in Palestine) had

Figure 1.1 Annual Rates of Growth of GDP and Private Consumption, 1951-1990 (constant prices)

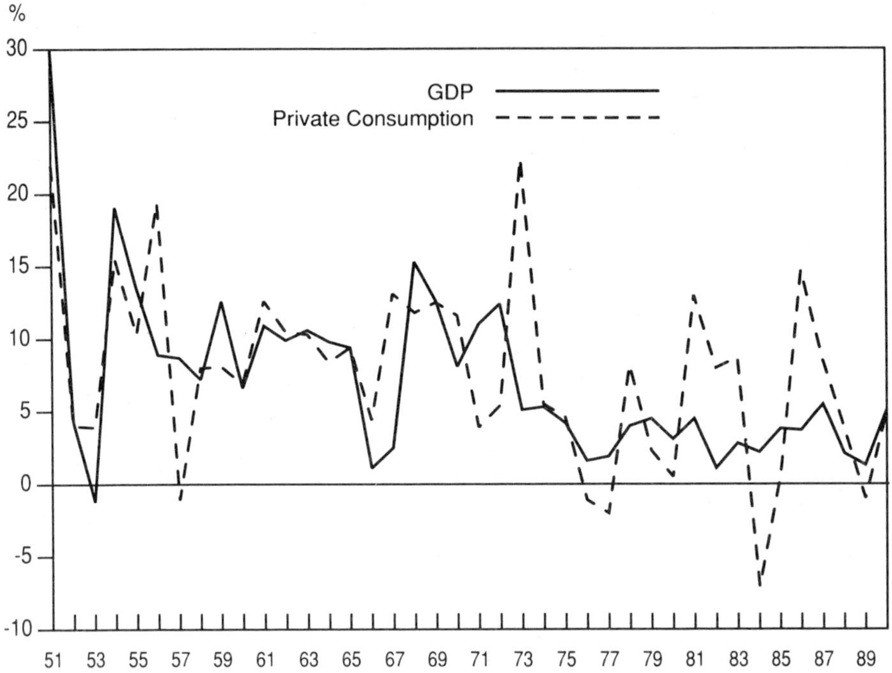

Source: Statistical Abstract of Israel 1990, Central Bureau of Statistics

important markets in the British military establishment in the Middle East. These markets contracted when the Second World War ended. Citrus was the economy's leading sector and provided most of the economy's exports. The disruption of the international citrus trade during the war also helped to turn many in the Yishuv against reliance on external trade. These pre-1948 experiences invoked a national ideology of self-sufficiency. After the declaration of independence in 1948, the country's socialist leadership favored minimal reliance on foreign sources of capital and revenues from trade in order to build an independent economy.

1948–1952: Austerity

In 1948 after the declaration of independence, Israel's economic prospects were bleak. The country was at war with all of its neighbors. After cease-fire agreements were signed Israel was subject to terrorist attacks from across its borders. In addition the first Arab-Israeli war of 1948–1949 provoked an exodus of Jews from Arab countries. As a result, 100,000

TABLE 1.1
Main Indicators of the Development of the Economy, 1981-1990
(annual percent change)

	1981-85	1986-87	1988	1989	1990
Sources	3.2	8.1	0.9	-1.4	6.3
GDP	2.9	4.8	2.7	1.6	5.1
Civilian imports (cif)	4.6	13.6	0.0	-1.1	7.0
Uses	3.2	8.1	0.9	-1.4	6.3
Private consumption	4.4	11.9	4.2	0.3	5.0
Public consumption (excluding direct defense imports)	1.5	0.3	3.6	0.6	1.9
Gross domestic investment	-0.1	5.9	-0.3	-5.3	25.2
Exports (fob)	5.2	8.4	-1.6	3.9	2.2
GDP of the business sector [a]	3.4	6.7	2.5	2.0	6.2
Rate of growth of population	1.7	1.6	1.6	1.9	5.5

[a] GDP of the business sector is equal to output of the whole economy less output from government, housing and non-profit making organizations.

Sources: 1981-1987: Annual Report 1989, Jerusalem: Bank of Israel, 1990; 1988-1990: Annual Report 1990, Jerusalem: Bank of Israel, 1991.

immigrants arrived in the country in the year of independence alone; over 200,000 arrived in 1949. The flow of immigrants was so large that only a bare minimum of support could be provided for them from public funds. Thousands were initially housed in tent encampments throughout the country before being moved into government-supplied huts.

The government's economic priority immediately after the war was to create work, but it lacked the necessary financial resources to achieve this objective. Loans were, therefore, taken from commercial banks through the sale of foreign exchange and government bonds. In addition money was printed, which resulted in inflationary pressures. These measures enabled the government to finance its basic activities and thus prevent a rise in unemployment. The latter came to only 6.7 percent of the labor force in 1950, a remarkably low figure given the large and sudden increase in the labor force.

Influenced by the success of wartime Britain's planned and tightly controlled economy, the government instituted a policy of austerity. Basic goods and services were rationed and controls were placed on the production of nonessential items. Such policies were in keeping with the egalitarian ideology that characterized the new state and its Labor-led government. They also seemed to be the only way to manage the pressures caused by war and mass immigration. Despite these measures, during the first few years after independence, there were widespread shortages in official markets and rapidly rising prices on increasingly important black markets, with deleterious effects on morale. But there were also achievements: A network of roads and thousands of housing units were built, and the government began to develop basic services such as postal delivery, telecommunications, railways, airlines, and radio broadcasting.

During the period before 1952 government policy attempted to achieve greater economic self-sufficiency. The emphasis of investment and settlement policy was agricultural; funds were channelled to new rural, agriculturally based communities. This policy, it was felt, would provide employment, food, and raw materials; agricultural settlement was also seen as a means of dispersing the population throughout the country. Furthermore, by the building of settlements in outlying and border areas, security was strengthened and the claim of the Jewish people to the land was enhanced. Because the private sector would be unlikely to invest in remote areas of the country, the logic of government action was reinforced.

In the area of foreign trade, government intervention was, by its very nature, better suited to preventing imports than encouraging exports. Imports could be easily controlled by administrative measures, whereas marketing exports abroad required the creation of companies with the necessary products and expertise, something that was beyond the government's capability. Hence, emphasis was placed on import substitution rather than exports as the driving force for growth in the economy. This emphasis applied to both industry and, where possible, agriculture.

1952–1972: From Stagnation to Rapid Economic Growth

1952: The First Moves Toward Liberalization

By 1952 the very tightly controlled economy was suffering serious shortages of foreign exchange and rising unemployment. In order to ease the foreign exchange constraint and provide funds for investment and thus employment, the first steps were taken toward economic liberalization. The government devalued the Israeli pound and took other measures to reduce inflation, cut the budget deficit, and improve the balance of payments. Price controls were also relaxed.

Financial pressures and a desire to increase the resources available for development were major factors leading to the decision to sign the Reparations Agreement with the Federal Republic of Germany in 1952. Designed to partially compensate Jews for the Holocaust, this arrangement provided for US$800 million to be paid to the Israeli government and Jewish institutions over the following twelve years. Another source of foreign currency was the sale of State of Israel bonds in the United States, which began at that time and was very successful.

The decision to raise capital abroad had important ideological and practical implications. Orthodox economic theory might suggest that at least part of Israel's underemployed labor force of the time would have best been employed in export industries set up by foreign investors. The latter would provide the technology, management, and marketing skills lacking in the economy. A deliberately undervalued exchange rate for the pound would encourage this development. However, policies of this kind ran counter to the political views of the government and the Histadrut (General Federation of Labor), which together dominated the country's economic and political life. They wanted to create well-paid jobs that provided a high standard of living so as to attract new immigrants in accordance with Zionist objectives. They did not favor reliance on the vagaries of foreign investors and international markets. By importing capital itself, the government was able to control a large part of the investment process and choose the sectors for development. It dominated the domestic capital market, borrowing from private savers to fund its deficit. This practice was not only a matter of financial necessity; there was an ideological preference for centralized direction in the allocation of resources. It is also doubtful that foreigners would have invested directly in the Israeli economy given the general risks involved at that time. The government, therefore, effectively became the guarantor of investments made by the private sector.

The improvement in the capital account of the balance of payments, as a result of the reparations agreements and the sale of bonds, was the major factor behind an acceleration of the economic growth rate. GNP rose by an annual average of nearly 17 percent in the period 1954–1955 compared to 1.8 percent in the period 1952–1953.[2]

The Economy in the 1960s and Early 1970s

During the late 1950s and early 1960s, with full employment and rapid economic growth, domestic costs rose. Exports of goods and services grew more slowly in volume terms than they had in the early and mid-1950s;

domestic demand squeezed them out. Imports rose more quickly and in February 1962 the minister of finance announced an economic stabilization program that included devaluation and a reduction in protective measures. The current account of the balance of payments had deteriorated because of a large growth of imports. In 1964 the excess of imports over exports was $464 million, a 43 percent increase over the previous year and a much higher level than had ever been experienced.[3] In 1965 the government once again decided on a policy of reducing demand in the economy in order to increase exports and reduce imports. Reparations payments from Germany had declined, as had foreign investment and other capital transfers. The economy relied increasingly on short-term borrowing. Anxiety about the foreign trade account also increased as France adopted a hostile policy toward Israel in negotiations on associate membership in the European Community (EC) (see Chapter 5). This hostility, it was felt, would threaten the development of trade links with the community.

These events led to a change in government policy that caused the economy to go into recession. The slowdown was deeper than originally contemplated: Growth of gross domestic product (GDP) slowed to about 2 percent a year in 1966 and 1967 compared with 10 percent in the previous five years. Growth of consumption and investment also decelerated and unemployment tripled between 1965 and 1967.

The Six-Day War of June 1967, however, changed the picture dramatically: As public sector demand (mainly from the defense sector) rose sharply, economic activity took an upward turn. The dramatic military victory produced a wave of optimism throughout the country that lasted until 1973. The victory of 1967 encouraged foreign investment and capital inflows. The GDP growth rate jumped to 15.3 percent in 1968; during the period 1969–1972 it averaged nearly 11 percent a year. This growth was made possible not only by an increased inflow of capital but also by a new supply of labor from the territories that had been captured in the war. In 1970 over 20,000 Arabs from these areas were working in Israel; by 1973 the number exceeded 60,000. There was also a significant increase in immigration from the West: 123,000 arrived between 1969 and 1972.[4] These immigrants brought both skills and capital and were rapidly integrated into the economy.

Factors Behind Rapid Growth

The rapid growth of the economy between 1948 and 1972 was largely the result of inflows of labor and capital. Between 1948 and 1973 the population of Israel increased from 870,000 to 3.3 million. Between 1974 and 1982 the population rose by 20 percent. Between 1983 and 1989 it increased by about 11 percent.

The civilian labor force more than doubled, from 450,000 in 1950 to 927,000 in 1967. In 1973 it reached 1.1 million. The skill and educational level of the labor force rose, despite large-scale immigration from developing countries, as a result of government training and educational programs. The growth of the other main factor of production, capital, was much greater. Between 1950 and 1967 the gross capital stock, measured in constant prices, increased eightfold. Output rose by 9.3 percent a year, while inputs increased by 5.9 percent a year.[5] All of these factors contributed to the large increase in productivity.

Almost all of the capital invested between 1948 and 1972 came from abroad; there was virtually no net domestic saving.[6] Although individuals and companies saved, the government borrowed from them in order to finance its deficit. The state's contribution was its organization of the inflow of capital from abroad. Inflows of labor and capital accounted for about 75 percent of the increase in GNP, the rest coming from increased efficiency in production.[7] This situation was a function of the stage of development: Management and technological change became more important than increases in the supply of labor and capital as development proceeded and the economy matured.

The fast rate of growth and high levels of defense spending resulted in balance-of-payments problems, even though capital imports usually exceeded the growing current account deficit. These capital imports were mainly preferential forms of finance; the scale of expensive, short-term borrowing on international markets was limited before 1973.

The structure of the economy, in terms of the share of different sectors, changed little between 1950 and 1967, despite rapid growth. There were, however, some changes within the period. The share of agriculture in national income rose from 11 percent in 1950 to 15 percent in 1958 but fell back to below 10 percent in 1966. Industry grew more slowly than other sectors in the early 1950s, but following a change in government policy and increased investment, growth of industrial output accelerated from 4.2 percent in the period 1950–1954 to 12.2 percent in the period 1955–1964. As industrial prices rose more rapidly than those of other sectors, industry's share in national income, on a current price basis, did not alter. Transport and communications increased their share with large-scale investment in the road network in the late 1950s. Increased construction followed the pattern of population growth, itself mainly a function of immigration. The level of construction activity was also related to the rise of living standards. The service sector accounted for over half of GDP throughout the period, reflecting the dominance of the state in the provision of social welfare and economic inputs.

Although the balance between sectors did not change very much, there were important developments within each sector. These developments led to rapid growth, which was the main characteristic of the economy in its first twenty-four years. Growth was made possible by large inflows of labor and capital and a gradual increase in educational and technological levels. Private consumption grew more slowly than output in most years, while public consumption grew more rapidly, using the savings of the private sector. The government was the main agency for economic development and was responsible, directly or indirectly, for the creation of much of Israel's industry in the period after 1954. In 1950 its expenditures accounted for 33 percent of GDP, in 1960 for 38 percent, and in 1970 for 65 percent.[8] The trend toward increased government spending mirrored that in the West: In the twenty-four Organization for Economic Cooperation and Development (OECD) countries, government spending as a share of GDP rose from 29 percent in 1960 to 41 percent in 1988.[9]

Despite many serious problems, the general picture in 1972 seemed very bright. The success of government policy during this period has been summarized in the following way: The successful absorption of large numbers of immigrants, the rapid growth of exports, the extensive increase in education, and the application of technology in agriculture practices all indicated that economic policy was effective.[10]

The Debate About Economic Policy

In the early 1960s a significant policy debate emerged about the liberalization and decentralization of the economy, echoes of which are still heard today. As the 1950s passed, the degree of import substitution declined. Attention began to focus on resource misallocation and the costs of protection. The debate took place between a group of economists at the Hebrew University, the Bank of Israel, and the Ministry of Finance, on the one hand, and a group at the Ministry of Industry and Trade, on the other. The former believed that the price mechanism was the best system for allocating resources and that government controls could not improve on its results. The economy had reached the point in its development at which the government could no longer act as central decision maker, allocating resources. The government should do no more than create a framework within which market forces would operate. The economic liberalizers advocated estimating a long-term equilibrium exchange rate by which the structure of production would be determined. The Ministry of Industry and Trade contended, in broad terms, that ideas of equilibria were applicable only in static situations and could not be applied to development problems, where structural changes were significant. With structural change, monopoly, and inevitable government involvement in the economy (if only because of the large defense budget), estimation of an equilibrium exchange rate was meaningless.

In 1962 the market-oriented proposals, involving an end to administrative controls on imports and a unification of the multiple exchange rate system, were adopted by the government, although their implementation took some years. Pressure from the Ministry of Agriculture delayed and eventually reduced the extent of the liberalization in agriculture and food processing. Implementation of the strategy was in the hands of a public committee consisting of representatives of the Ministries of Finance and Industry, the Histadrut, and the Manufacturers' Association (the Federation of Employers). The Ministry of Industry often supported the arguments of those wanting continued protection. The result was that the costs and benefits of each case were analyzed separately, rather than on an overall basis, and by 1968 liberalization applied to only 50 percent of manufactured output.[11] A similar debate is now going on regarding restrictions and taxes on imports currently in force. This debate is analyzed in greater detail in Chapter 5.

Foreign Trade and Capital Imports

The current account deficit fell sharply as a share of national income between 1950 and 1960 because exports increased more rapidly than imports. It widened again in the 1960s in part because greater emphasis on exports increased their level of sophistication and also their import content, which resulted in higher import levels.

Exports, in current dollars, increased by a factor of sixteen between 1950 and 1967; their composition also changed as traditional commodities such as citrus and diamonds became less important while those of other industries and services increased their share. Exports suffered for much of the period from an overvalued exchange rate and low standards of technology, especially aging machinery. Costs were high because Israel was a long distance from its markets and sources of raw materials. Government assistance took the form of cheap credits for the purchase of capital equipment and export incentives. Although the volume of exports grew dramatically, it did so from a low base. The profitability of exports was often not high enough to persuade firms to sell abroad, as was especially true during the 1965–1967 recession.

The economy became increasingly open to international trade: Imports tripled in dollar terms between 1950 and 1967, constituting 30 percent of GNP in 1950 and 35 percent in 1967. As the economy developed, the share of consumer goods in total imports fell from 26 percent in the period 1949–1952 to 10 percent in the period 1965–1966. The development of the economy and particularly of industry increased the need for capital goods. Increasingly sophisticated industrial products had a greater import content; as a result imports rose.

Despite the fact that economic policy came under increasing criticism, the economy grew at rates achieved by few other countries, and the government succeeded in maintaining full employment. The protectionist policies of the 1950s were not critically harmful to the country's increased integration into the world economy during the following two decades.[12]

In its first twenty years, Israel imported about $7 billion in medium-term and long-term capital. Approximately 70 percent of this capital consisted of transfers, including German reparations, and personal and institutional remittances. Thirty percent was loans and investments, including about 10 percent from the sale of Israeli government bonds abroad.

Gradually the emphasis of policy changed. Importing capital, although still considered important, was set alongside the need to rationalize its use by relying more on market forces. As a result, by 1967, the economy had made the significant move from administrative protection (quantitative restrictions on imports) to tariffs (import duties). This change meant that prices, rather than the government, became the dominant influence on what could be imported. After 1975, in accordance with agreements with the EC, most of these tariffs on EC goods were reduced and at the end of 1988 they were finally abolished. Quotas were retained and played an increased role until their abolition in 1991 (see Chapter 5).

Foreign trade liberalization moves did not resolve balance-of-payments problems. There was a current account deficit every year from 1948 to 1972; in order to finance this deficit Israel had to obtain unilateral transfers (gifts) or borrow abroad. As a result, there were, in the short run, more resources available to the economy than those provided by GDP. The excess, insofar as it was not provided by grants and gifts from abroad, was financed by debt. The extra resources borrowed in one year were paid for with interest payments in subsequent years. Although exports paid for an increasing share of the import bill, the absolute size of the trade gap grew. As a result of economic growth, however, the share of the deficit in GDP remained remarkably constant over a long period (see Table 1.1).

During the 1960s Israel's imports began to be partly financed by loans. The investments made possible by the import surplus were not profitable enough to fund repayment of the loans, and part of the extra resources went into consumption. Hence, the debt grew faster than the economy's ability to finance it, and the import surplus became a burden on future generations.[13]

1973: A Fateful Year

The Yom Kippur War, which broke out in October 1973, resulted in the death of 3,000 Israeli soldiers and the wounding of many more. It also marked a watershed in economic performance. Between 1973 and 1985 the economy was buffeted by a series of crises that lowered economic growth rates, worsened the balance of payments, and caused spiralling inflation. The Yom Kippur War itself was the first blow; it was immediately followed by a rise in international oil prices.

During 1973 the economy began to face problems from which it has still not recovered. Increasing oil prices and other import costs as well as the international recession had deleterious effects on the economy. As a result, economic growth declined and the balance of payments deteriorated. Short-term, expensive loans were taken to finance the deficit, which in turn increased the foreign debt and interest payments abroad.

The cost of the Yom Kippur War may have equalled over 75 percent of that year's GNP of $9.2 billion. It is not possible to define the period over which this cost was borne. During 1973 imports of defense goods increased sharply, as did public consumption. Defense expenditure increased in real terms by 66 percent compared with 1972. Disruption of the economy and the call-up of reservists, many of whom were still in uniform in the spring of 1974, affected exports and production. The United States assisted Israel with the foreign currency costs of the war (increased arms imports), but only from 1976 did this assistance fully cover the costs of direct defense imports.

Although in 1973 a secular decline occurred in the growth rate of the national income, it still remained higher than the OECD average. In 1974 and 1975 this rate reflected in part the high levels of government expenditure on defense. There was a slowdown in 1976 and 1977 as economic policy became more deflationary, but Israel's adjustment to the era of high oil prices and international recession was belated and therefore costly.

The Increased Cost of Oil

Increases in the international price of oil had their effect on Israel soon after the war. At the end of 1973, the country was paying $130 per ton for oil on spot markets. As a result of the Arab boycott, Israel was unable to obtain supplies under contract and consequently had to pay double the price paid by those who had contracts with Middle Eastern oil suppliers. Under the terms of the Second Disengagement Agreement with Egypt, Israel evacuated most of the Sinai oil fields in 1976. Most of Israel's oil then had to be imported at high prices on international markets. For these reasons a guarantee of oil supplies was obtained from the United States. The oil import bill rose from $98 million in 1972 to $628 million in 1975 and $1.8 billion in 1980. Between 1973 and 1982, the deterioration in the terms of trade, largely a result of the increase in the international price of oil, has been estimated to have cost Israel $12 billion.[14]

Increases in oil prices were abrupt and caused inflationary pressures. Between mid-1973 and 1975 energy price increases accounted for about one-third of the acceleration in inflation; in 1980 inflation would have been 100 percent rather than 130 percent if oil prices had not risen on international markets. Israel's exposure to the effects of international oil price changes was intensified by the extent of the country's reliance on it as a source of energy. Only in 1974 was the decision made to construct the first power station that could use coal as well as oil. This station began operation in 1982, after Israel had withdrawn from the remaining oil fields in the Sinai, which since 1976 had supplied 25 percent of its oil needs.

Increased oil consumption per unit of GNP and the factors described above combined to increase the ratio of energy imports to GNP from 1 percent in the 1950s and 1960s to 4.6 percent in 1974 and 12 percent in 1979. The development of the petro-chemical industry increased demand for oil as a production input: The decision to develop this industry was made before 1973 and it contributed to a doubling of feedstock demand between 1974 and 1980. After 1980 the fuel bill fell as international prices came down. By 1985 the cost of fuel was $1.5 billion, 17 percent less in current dollar terms than in 1980.

Some Broader Implications of the 1973 War

The Yom Kippur War had important effects on Israeli society as well as on the economy; it also affected political decision making. After public protests against the lack of preparedness for and the misconduct of the war, Prime Minister Golda Meir resigned. She was the last of the founding generation of the state to lead the government. The new government formed by the Labor party, under Yitzhak Rabin, undertook the difficult task of adjusting the economy to the harsh realities of the post–Yom Kippur War period.

The changes in the political leadership were superficial; in reality the Labor leadership had suffered a collapse in political power and vision. The government existed more on a day-to-day basis than before, dealing with crises in many sectors almost simultaneously. The sense of unity and purpose that had characterized Israel until the 1970s faded as domestic division increased and the founding fathers of the Labor movement died or retired (see Chapter 7).

Economic Policy, 1973–1980

1973–1977: Restraint and Reform

The period immediately after 1973 was an extremely difficult one for the economy. The war had caused massive disruption and used up huge quantities of resources against a background of rapidly increasing oil costs. GDP per capita grew by 1 percent a year between 1974 and 1977. Investment fell by an average of 4.7 percent a year and export growth slumped until 1976.

In November 1974, the exchange rate was devalued by 43 percent, existing subsidies were cut, an import surcharge was imposed, and export subsidies were introduced. Fuel, water, and electricity prices were increased, all part of an austerity program. The government had to meet rising debt repayments and defense costs.

Consumer prices rose by 39.7 percent in 1974 to double their 1973 rate and over triple their 1972 rate. This increase far exceeded the inflation rate of countries with which Israel conducted most of its trade. Devaluations were therefore needed in order to maintain competitiveness. Anticipation of the 1974 devaluation led to capital inflows, which had inflationary effects. In June 1975 a system of so-called crawling peg devaluations was introduced with the aim of improving the balance of payments without causing domestic instability. (The implications of these changes are examined in Chapters 2 and 5.)

Private consumption grew much faster than GDP in the period 1973–1976. This increase was also true on a per capita basis; it reflected the inability and unwillingness of the government to adopt even tougher measures. In 1975 the government implemented the recommendations of a commission on income tax reform. It indexed tax brackets to changes in the consumer price index and sharply increased their real value. A wide range of tax exemptions were abolished; nearly all wage earnings became subject to taxation at the same rate. These reforms constituted a major improvement in the tax system and were one of the major economic achievements of the period.

The 1977 General Elections

The general elections of 1977 marked a turning point in Israel's political history: Labor lost office after twenty-nine years in power. Reasons for this change included anxieties about the 1973 war and resentment of the long-term Labor government among many Sephardi Jews (Jews of North African and Middle Eastern origin) because of their relatively low status and income compared to those of European origin. The Labor party had become divided and corrupt; its leadership no longer inspired the people. Finally, there had been a continuous shift to the right in some sections of public opinion on security and defense issues, which was reflected in the defection of the National Religious party from its traditional parliamentary alliance with Labor to the nationalist Likud. This move ultimately enabled Menachem Begin, the Likud leader, to form the new government.

The Likud comprised two sections. Herut was the main nationalist party, whose major concerns lay in defense and foreign policy. The much smaller Liberal party was mainly interested in economic issues: It wanted to reduce government control and reduce the power of the Histadrut. Herut drew its support from the traditional nationalist section of the population and from Sephardi Jews who had become increasingly hostile to the Labor establishment. The Liberals added a small constituency of those in the middle class who supported the nationalist message of their senior partners in the Likud.

After the election, the Liberals gained the Finance Ministry. Simcha Ehrlich was appointed minister, and he started working on plans for economic reform. The concomitant of the Liberals' policies (which stressed efficiency, sale of public companies, and less government intervention) was a cut in government expenditure. This policy, however, came into conflict with the populist policies of the Herut. The electoral strength of the latter lay in part with the underprivileged, who would suffer from expenditure cuts. As will be seen, these tensions had profound effects on the economic policies of the Likud government between 1977 and 1984.

Another reason budgetary restraint became so hard to achieve was the commitment of the new government to expand Jewish settlement in the West Bank and Gaza. These settlements were the subject of intense international criticism and much domestic debate. From a narrow, economic point of view, they represented a spreading of the national development effort over a wider geographical area. Both the Galilee and the Negev continued to be underdeveloped and their chances of receiving adequate funding receded during this period. The cost of the settlement program was high: It is estimated to have equalled 2.75 percent of GNP in 1981–1982.[15]

1977–1980: Liberalization

Liberalizing the economy through exchange rate and foreign trade reform was not just a matter for the Liberal party and its finance minister. Many of the officials in the Ministry of Finance and the Bank of Israel, with whom the minister worked, had for years been associated with the Labor governments of 1948–1977. They had formulated and implemented the liberalizations of that period and saw the 1977 reform as part of a comprehensive package of measures designed to make the economy more efficient. Hence the governor of the Bank of Israel, in his introduction to the Bank's 1977 *Annual Report,* stated that the foreign currency reform made economic policy more effective but that it was not a substitute for fiscal policies and other policies to control increases in prices and incomes.[16]

At the end of October 1977, the shekel was devalued by 47 percent, travel taxes were abolished, foreign exchange controls were eased, customs duties were reduced, and other measures were introduced to liberalize the exchange and payments systems. One of the most important steps taken was to permit Israelis to buy assets linked to foreign currencies, which were thus protected against devaluations. Before the liberalization, only those involved in foreign trade, those in banking, recipients of foreign incomes, new immigrants, and nonresidents could hold such assets.

The October 1977 devaluation was not, however, accompanied by reductions in domestic expenditure. During 1978–1979, government expenditure increased by 1 percent compared with a fall of 22 percent in 1976–1977. There was a similar pattern in investment, which rose by nearly 15 percent in 1978–1979 compared with a fall of 18.6 percent in 1976–1977. In addition, in the two years after the October 1977 devaluation, private consumption rose by 16.5 percent in real terms, compared with 9.8 percent in 1976–1977.

In November 1977 President Anwar Sadat of Egypt made his historic journey to Jerusalem and peace talks between Israel and Egypt began. In 1979 a peace treaty was signed and Israel began to withdraw its military installations and armed forces from the Sinai. The cost of moving hardware and equipment and building new military bases was considerable. It led to an increase in defense expenditure just when the defense burden needed to be substantially reduced in order to lower aggregate demand and make room for exports.

As a result of high domestic demand, exports rose in volume terms by only 8 percent in 1978–1979 compared with 29 percent in 1976–1977; imports, however, increased by 14 percent in 1978–1979 compared with a fall of 5.5 percent during the latter period. This pattern was exactly the opposite of what was required for a successful devaluation. Exchange rate and foreign trade liberalization is usually aimed, inter alia, at improving the trade balance. The gains that had been achieved by deflationary policies between 1974 and 1977 were being lost. A deficit on goods and services of $4 billion in 1975 had been reduced to $2.6 billion in 1977, but by 1979 it worsened to $3.9 billion.

The most dramatic effect of the 1977 policy changes was an upsurge in inflation that lasted until 1985. Consumer prices rose by 34.6 percent in 1977 and 78.3 percent in 1978. The increase was in large part due to the devaluation, which increased import costs; these were easily passed on to consumers because of the buoyant demand in the economy. The system of indexation, which linked increases in wages to those in the cost-of-living index, ensured that price rises were passed through the economy, with wages increasing in compensation (see Chapter 3). This situation made it difficult to reduce purchasing power. Domestic demand was not squeezed to make room for more exports and reduce imports. Growth of GDP accelerated from 2.0 percent in 1976–1977 to 4.5 percent in 1978–

1979, but insofar as it was only a result of increased consumption, it was to be a temporary upswing.

November 1979 to January 1981: Restraint Again

In November 1979 Finance Minister Ehrlich was replaced by Yigal Horovitz. The new minister rapidly introduced a series of deflationary measures designed to improve balance of payments and reduce inflation. Consumer subsidies and allocations of interest-free credit were cut. Electricity prices and those of other public utilities rose, and the deposits with the government that were payable on imports were increased. Much construction activity was frozen, as were public service employee hirings. Income tax as a share of average salaries rose from 14 percent in 1978 to 19 percent in 1980. Revenues from income tax increased by 14.7 percent in real terms in 1979. These were measures taken by the Finance Ministry; at the same time the Bank of Israel tightened monetary policy in an attempt to reduce the inflationary effects of capital inflows attracted by high interest rates. Civilian public consumption was reduced by 1.2 percent in 1980 compared with an increase of 2 percent in 1979, but the effects of this change were undermined by increases in defense expenditures; as a result total government consumption rose by 9.1 percent.

Horovitz's policies, which were accompanied by strong calls to the public to reduce its consumption and adopt a regime of austerity, helped to improve the balance of payments. Between 1979 and 1980 total exports of goods and services rose by 20.4 percent in dollar terms while imports rose by 8.5 percent. The civilian deficit fell from $1.9 billion to $1.2 billion; industrial exports rose by 25 percent.

Private consumption fell by 2.7 percent in 1980 after an 8 percent rise in 1979; investment fell by 13.3 percent. These changes helped to reduce imports and make room for exports. Balance-of-payments improvements were not matched by reduced inflation: The latter accelerated from 111 percent in 1979 to 133 percent in 1980. Accelerating inflation became a major cause of public anxiety and led to a change in economic policy.

The Economy in the Early 1980s

1981–1983: Populism and Crisis

Elections were due in the spring of 1981; the finance minister wanted to maintain restrictive economic policies despite their lack of popularity. The Cabinet refused to back him and overturned his rejection of a proposed teachers' pay increase. Yigal Horovitz resigned in January 1981. His successor, Yoram Aridor, immediately introduced radically different policies. He reduced taxes and increased subsidies in expectation of increased consumer expenditure that would yield higher tax revenues. The rate of devaluation of the shekel was also slowed. The new minister's policies, which increased the public's purchasing power, helped to bring about the reelection of the Likud government in June 1981 and have affected the economy ever since.

The change of finance ministers represented the triumph of populism over liberalism and austerity. The loosening of financial controls before the election was not without precedent, but the preelection tax cuts and subsidy increases continued after the election and were on a scale never before experienced.

1983–1984: Inflation Accelerates

With the resignation in October 1983 of Yoram Aridor, the fourth Likud finance minister, Yigal Cohen-Orgad, came to office. (The economic events surrounding Aridor's resignation are examined in Chapter 2.) Cohen-Orgad began a program of deflationary measures and devalued the shekel, but as general elections were scheduled for the summer of 1984, economic policy was quickly reversed again. Taxes were cut, subsidies increased, and consequently inflation accelerated. The details of the steps taken after the general election are examined in the following chapter.

Notes

1. *Statistical Abstract of Israel* (Jerusalem: Central Bureau of Statistics, 1986), p. 171.
2. Ibid.
3. C. S. Greenwood, *Recession as a Policy Instrument: Israel 1965–69* (London: C. Hurst & Co., 1972).
4. *Statistical Abstract of Israel* (Jerusalem: Central Bureau of Statistics, 1974).
5. M. Bruno, "Economic Development Problems of Israel," in C. A. Cooper and S. A. Alexander, eds., *Economic Development and Population Growth in the Middle East* (New York: American Elsevier, 1972).
6. Ibid.
7. Ibid.
8. J. Arnon, "Forty Years of the Israeli Economy," *Economic Quarterly*, vol. 138 (Tel Aviv, November 1988). In Hebrew.
9. *Economist* (London), 7 January 1988.
10. C. A. Cooper and S. A. Alexander, *Economic Development*, Introduction.
11. R. Pomfret, *Trade Policies and Industrialization in a Small Country: The Case of Israel* (Tubingen: JCB Mohr/Paul Siebert, 1976).
12. Ibid.
13. D. Patinkin, *The Israeli Economy: The First Decade* (Jerusalem: Maurice Falk Institute for Economic Research in Israel, 1967).

14. Z. Sussman, *Stagnation, Inflation and the Balance of Payments: Can the Performance of the Israeli Economy Be Improved?* (Tel Aviv: Jacob Levinson Center of the Israel-Diaspora Institute, and London: Institute for Jewish Affairs, July 1985).

15. J. Arnon, *Economy in Turmoil* (Tel Aviv: Hakibbutz Hameuchad, 1985). In Hebrew.

16. *Annual Report 1977* (Jerusalem: Bank of Israel, May 1978). In Hebrew.

2

Inflation and the Loss of Economic Control

The Acceleration of Inflation in the Late 1970s and Early 1980s

From 1979 until 1985 hyperinflation caused serious economic problems, the consequences of which are still being felt. It destroyed the normal operation of the price mechanism, and after 1980, it became the central issue in economic policy. The 1970s began with relatively low but accelerating inflation and ended with prices rising by more than 100 percent a year. By 1984 prices were rising at an annual rate of 445 percent (see Figure 2.1).

The origins of these problems can be found in the economic policy development of the 1970s. Between 1960/61 and 1973/74, as the economy moved from recession to boom, the government deficit as a share of gross national product (GNP) rose from virtually zero to a peak of 16 percent. Between 1970 and 1972 the deficit averaged $1 billion, in 1973 it more than doubled to $2.3 billion, and by 1974 it had reached $3.3 billion.[1] These massive increases had several causes; the primary reason was the rise in defense expenditures, which will be examined in Chapter 3. There were also significant rises in social service spending, subsidies, transfers to individuals and firms, and interest payments; interest payments were largely the result of borrowing in previous years. Between fiscal years 1977/78 and 1984/85 spending on these items rose by 110 percent in dollar terms. As the spending was not matched by higher revenues, the deficit grew to levels far exceeding those of Organization for Economic Cooperation and Development (OECD) countries. Inflation in the mid-1970s was sustained by government deficits against a background of full employment.[2] Between 1973/74 and 1978/79 the deficit fell but inflation increased.

In the early 1980s there were significant changes in the way the deficit was financed. In 1980/81, 72.5 percent of the deficit (including interest

Figure 2.1 Inflation: Annual Increase in the Consumer Price Index, 1975-1990

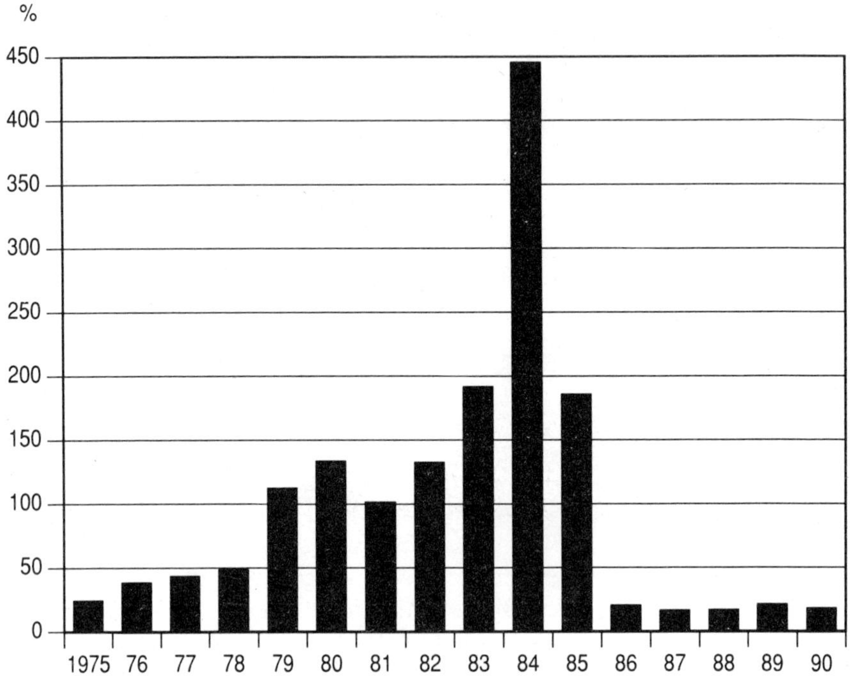

Source: Price Statistics Monthly, Central Bureau of Statistics

payments) was funded by borrowing from the public, 17.4 percent by printing money, and 10.1 percent by government sales to the public of assets, whose values were linked to the exchange rate. By 1984/85 borrowing accounted for only 32 percent of the deficit while printing money accounted for 20.4 percent and sales of foreign currency 47.6 percent. It is significant that long-term borrowing from the public fell from a monthly average of 4 percent of GNP in 1982 to minus 1 percent in 1984.[3] This decrease reflected the public's unwillingness to lend funds to the government; it did not feel that it would be adequately rewarded by interest and inflation compensation. The public increasingly preferred short-term deposits linked to the exchange rate of the shekel, which were known as Patam, that could easily be encashed. Liquid assets as a share of total assets rose from 22.3 percent in 1982 to 31.2 percent in 1984.[4]

In order to improve the balance of payments, major devaluations were carried out in 1971 (20 percent) and in 1974 (43 percent). The rate of exchange was then fixed, but the effect of the adjustment was transitory, and soon after the devaluation, inflation was back to its previous levels, wiping out the competitive gain. With the introduction of the so-called crawling peg exchange rate mechanism in June 1975, which took the form of a 2 percent monthly devaluation, inflation exceeded the level of price rises in Israel's trading partners by the rate of devaluation.

According to research carried out at the Bank of Israel, in the years prior to 1975, expectations of price rises were influenced by events in the relatively distant past.[5] People reacted on the basis of what they remembered had happened in previous years. The crawling peg exchange rate considerably reduced the lag in adjusting expectations, and so reactions to recent and more rapidly changing events now took place. Nominal changes in the economy occurred more rapidly, which caused the public to react with ever greater speed. The crawling peg was a mechanism that permitted inflation to continue: Everyone knew that wage and price rises would rapidly be followed by a devaluation that would restore the economy's competitiveness to the level that prevailed before domestic costs rose.

The 1977 liberalization intensified this process by permitting the public to buy assets linked to the exchange rate for various foreign currencies. It was accompanied by a 47 percent devaluation, which increased the price level and the value, in local currency, of assets indexed to the consumer price index and the exchange rate. Between 1979 and 1981 the government reduced the extent to which it lent funds on an unlinked basis. This kind of lending, mainly for housing mortgages, substantially added to the budget deficit.

In 1981 measures were taken that increased the level of demand in the economy and added to inflationary pressures: Subsidies rose from $550 million in 1980 to $1.5 billion in 1981; indirect taxes, especially on imported consumer durables, were reduced; the lag in the adjustment of income tax brackets to inflation was eliminated; and transfer payments rose.[6] The aim of this policy was to reduce inflationary expectations by reducing prices and thereby moderate wage demands. Implicit was the view that changing expectations would reduce inflation. Increased spending on consumer durables would, the government believed, increase its revenues and thus help to reduce the budget deficit. In fact the opposite occurred: The deficit jumped from 8 percent of GNP in 1980 to 14 percent in 1981.

In June 1982, with the outbreak of the war in Lebanon, taxes were increased in an attempt to reduce the budget deficit or at least slow its growth. The increase in taxation was only the first in a series of policy reversals that themselves increased uncertainty and instability. By the autumn of 1982 anxiety was mounting about the acceleration of inflation from an annual rate of 102 percent to 158 percent. The Bank of Israel stated that there had been a huge increase in the government's budget deficit that was due to higher defense spending and civilian consumption. This change had not been accompanied by a commensurate growth of net taxes (their weight in gross domestic product [GDP] remained unchanged) and had led to both a higher rate of inflation and a large drop in public sector saving.[7]

As well as limiting devaluations to 5 percent a month, the government restricted increases in prices of controlled commodities to the same rate, despite a much higher underlying rate of inflation. This meant that subsidies rose, increasing the budget deficit.

By July 1983 the shekel had to be devalued by an extra 7 percent in addition to the regular adjustment. The public no longer believed that the government could maintain the artificially high exchange rate, which had brought about a cumulative deterioration in Israel's external competitiveness of 32 percent between 1981 and 1983. In May 1983 the Bank of Israel drew attention to the collapse of the economic policy and foreshadowed the crisis of October 1983:

> It had recently become customary to attribute an important role to inflationary expectations in explaining the rise of prices. The success of the policies pursued between 1981 and the beginning of 1983 was largely due to moderation of these expectations, but the frequent changes of policy and the stressing of the income side were not conducive to creating a feeling that price advantage would be retained. The public evidently did not believe that the government would persist in these measures for any length of time.[8]

In the period up to 1980, sales of foreign exchange to the public were used to stabilize the exchange rate rather than to control the money supply. Exchange rate policy and open market operations in foreign exchange were instruments for reducing the import surplus.[9] From the period 1980–1982 policy changed: Sales of foreign exchange were made in order to cover the budget deficit and to maintain a stable exchange rate.

Most public debt consisted of government bonds, linked to the consumer price index and sold in unlimited quantities at positive real rates of interest. Sales were used to stabilize the real rate of return on public debt, helping to ensure that the government could meet its financing requirements. Some bonds were linked to the exchange rate; their volume depended on public demand. Their rate of return depended on the exchange rate and international interest rates, which could not be manipulated to control the money supply.

In this situation changes in the money supply magnified and prolonged price shocks in the system, which affected inflationary expectations and were an important, negative effect of devaluations. Indexation meant that price increases in one sector were transferred to others. Rapid inflation increased the speed of adjustment and shortened the lag between present price experience and changes in inflationary expectations. As a result acceleration of price inflation preceded accelerations of monetary growth.

During 1983 the public further increased its purchases of foreign currency. It was able to do this by selling bank shares, the values of which were rising sharply as a result of the banks' support of their share prices (see Chapter 6). The public understood the implications of deteriorating balance-of-payments figures and acted to protect itself against a devaluation, which its very actions had helped to make inevitable.

In October 1983 the shekel was devalued by 23 percent and allowed to float on a daily basis. The finance minister, Yoram Aridor, who had proposed linking the shekel to the dollar as a means of simultaneously reducing inflation and improving the balance of payments, resigned. His so-called dollarization plan was seen as a gimmick that would bring to an end the country's economic independence. His resignation was a reflection of the disastrous consequences of the economic policies he had introduced. The government then took steps to protect the balance of payments and permitted inflation to increase: Subsidies were reduced in autumn 1983 but prior to the general election, in summer 1984, were increased again. During 1984 there was a major improvement in the balance of payments, due in large part to a fast growth of exports. This improvement was partly the result of a rapid but short-lived expansion of world trade. However, it was not large or rapid enough to prevent the foreign exchange reserves from falling in 1985, thus causing a major crisis.

The elections of July 1984 resulted in a deadlock between the two major political parties and their allies in the Knesset. In September a government of National Unity was formed by Labor and the Likud along with some of their allies. The new government immediately devalued the shekel, reduced subsidies, and introduced restrictions on imports. Inflation accelerated from annual rates of 311 percent in the first quarter of 1984 to 496 percent in the second and 536 percent in the third.

In an attempt to reduce inflation, a three-month wage and price freeze was introduced from November 1984 to the end of January 1985. The Histadrut agreed to forgo compensation for wage erosion in return for a freeze on the prices of subsidized goods and on formerly uncontrolled goods and services. The freeze reduced the rate of inflation but not the underlying pressures, partly because the government had to increase its spending on subsidies. At the end of the freeze, prices rose sharply, and after subsidy cuts another freeze was introduced at the beginning of February 1985. It was supplanted by a third freeze, which was supposed to last for six months. Producers were to absorb part of the increase in their costs, workers to forgo part of the cost-of-living adjustments related to increases in the prices of subsidized goods. Reductions in subsidies were aimed at cutting the budget deficit. This was a voluntary package and that very fact helped to undermine it.

The underlying reason these measures failed was that they were supported by high levels of government expenditure, financed in large part by inflationary mechanisms. The floating exchange rate increased the price of imports and in turn contributed to inflationary pressures.

The Economic Stabilization Program of July 1985

By June 1985 it had become clear that inflation could not be reduced more than temporarily by wage and price freezes. Improvement in the trade deficit, which had occurred in 1984, faded in 1985. Most worrying was a fall in the foreign exchange reserves to what were considered dangerously low levels, which finally provoked major policy changes.

At the beginning of July, at an all-night Cabinet meeting, the government adopted a comprehensive plan to stabilize the economy. Its aim was to improve the balance of payments and reduce inflation simultaneously. The program involved an immediate 18.8 percent devaluation of the shekel and a subsequent freezing of its rate against the dollar. (This freeze lasted until February 1987.) The prices of subsidized goods were increased by between 35 percent and 75 percent while nonsubsidized items went up by 17 percent. This was followed by a freeze on prices. Employees were only to be partly compensated for the erosion of wages; an agreement to this effect was signed on July 15. The government, having unilaterally declared its intention of introducing a state of emergency, suspended cost-of-living allowance agreements. The cost-of-living agreements would have brought an 18 percent increase in wages and salaries in August in order to compensate for 80 percent of the rise in prices that had occurred in May and June. Compensation for the July price rises (which came to 27.5 percent) would have been paid at the beginning of September under the old agreement. Instead, a 14 percent payment in August and a 12 percent payment in September were agreed to. This agreement followed pressure from the Histadrut, which declared a one-day national strike on July 2. Real gross wages at the beginning of August were 7 percent below their July 1 level, and at the beginning of September they were 18 percent lower. During this period tax thresholds increased sharply in real terms as a result of the slowdown in inflation. Income tax brackets were linked to the price index of the previous quarter; as inflation slowed in the autumn, taxpayers gained the benefit of linkage to the price rises of the early summer.

The budgetary measures were designed to reduce the deficit by $1.5 billion, thus offsetting the increases in the 1985/86 budget that had occurred in its first three months. The government proposed to cut $250 million from its expenditures on goods and services and to dismiss 10,000 public sector workers. Its spending would also be reduced by the erosion of gross wages. Other changes included a restriction on the purchase of foreign currency–linked assets to those with maturity of less than a year.

The most important aspect of the program was the simultaneity of the measures. According to one of the authors of the plan, the most important single element was the cut in the budget deficit. Although the original proposals only pushed spending back to its March 1985 level, this move was a start on a road toward reducing the size of the public sector.[10] The next item of importance was the freezing of the exchange rate at a competitive level. The exchange rate, in a small, open economy suffering from hyperinflation, was an important price "anchor." It affected inflation and was the basis for many asset prices in the linkage system. The public followed movements in the exchange rate as a guide to the value of its assets and as an indication of government policy and of the state of the economy. Freezing the exchange rate would provide a basis for holding down prices, nominal wages, and costs throughout the economy.

Against this background the system of indexation would be broken by granting only partial compensation for price rises and delaying payments for these purposes. These moves would lower wage costs and thus increase the economy's competitiveness in the face of both inflation still in the system and a frozen exchange rate.

Monetary policy had to provide people with an incentive to hold on to local currency and assets denominated in shekels rather than to buy black market dollars and assets denominated in foreign currency. This incentive was achieved with the aid of a very large increase in interest rates, which caused financial difficulties for the productive sectors of the economy.

The government sought and received emergency aid from the United States in order to bolster the foreign exchange reserves. This aid improved the capital account of the balance of payments and reduced the need to borrow on expensive, short-term money markets abroad.

The program was very successful in reducing inflation. In the second month of its operation prices were rising more slowly than they had for over three years. In November 1985 the monthly inflation rate was less than 1 percent, and the price level actually fell in January 1986. In the six months from August 1985 through January 1986, prices rose by 12.6 percent compared to 136 percent in the previous half year.

Reducing inflation was not the only aim of the program but it was by far the most successful. Also in 1985, an improvement occurred in the balance of payments, but this was partly due to a trend whose origins preceded the July program. The July measures were greatly assisted by the fall in the value of the dollar against the major European currencies, which lowered Israel's import costs while reducing its export prices in Europe. The fall in international oil prices also reduced costs and helped to improve the current account of the balance of payments. Large-scale U.S. emergency economic assistance provided an element of financial stability and acted as a foreign vote of confidence in the program.

Major changes occurred in the state budget during the summer of 1985. Subsidies were drastically reduced, other expenditures were more modestly cut or frozen, and taxes were steeply increased. The effect was to reduce the budget deficit (excluding interest payments) from 9 percent in 1984 to 2 percent in 1985 (see Table 2.1). The reduction of subsidies to industry, agriculture, and parts of the service sector was of long-term significance (see Chapters 4 and 8). From 1985 on, many companies and economic entities such as cooperatives and kibbutzim began to suffer serious economic difficulties. They had all relied on cheap government credits, many of which suddenly dried up and were also subject to a massive rise in real interest rates, which occurred almost overnight. Nominal interest rates rose in 1984, but when inflation fell in the second half of 1985, real interest rates jumped. The real interest rate on nondirected, short-term local currency credits, which financed production for the local market, reached 100 percent in the second half of 1985. For nearly thirty years, reliance on the government (especially for cheap credit) was an accepted way of doing business; suddenly the rules of the game had changed. It took several years for this new reality to be absorbed by those concerned and the effects are still being felt.

Economic Analysis Behind the 1985 Program

From the early 1970s until 1985 the government attempted to achieve real devaluations in order to improve the balance of payments and increase economic growth. The theory behind these policies was that a devaluation in excess of local inflation would lower the price abroad of Israeli exports in relation to nontraded goods in the economy. It would also reduce the demand for imports by increasing their relative price. In order for such a policy to succeed, the government had to control or, if possible, reduce spending and wages in the economy to make room for exports. It had to strengthen incentives to sell abroad rather than at home. If local demand was relatively weak (because of deflationary policies accompanying a devaluation), then the chances of exports rising were greater than if local demand was strong.

These policies did not work during this period, however. Exports increased in 1980 and 1984 partly because of reductions in domestic demand in 1979 and 1983, but the export growth trend was weak in the first half of the decade. Economic growth was not sustained and the

TABLE 2.1
The Budget Deficit and Its Financing, 1980-1985
(percent of GDP, monthly averages, including payments to the Bank of Israel)

	1980	1981	1982	1983	1984	1985
Components of deficit						
Domestic expenditure	51.0	53.8	54.1	51.5	50.0	48.5
Taxes	44.7	44.0	47.5	48.1	40.9	46.6
Deficit excluding interest	6.3	9.8	6.6	3.4	9.0	1.9
Interest	7.0	2.6	4.3	3.4	4.4	6.3
Domestic deficit	13.3	12.4	10.9	6.8	13.4	8.2
Finance of deficit						
Base money creation	2.1	2.1	1.8	2.4	3.1	6.8
Domestic net debt [a]	6.5	8.7	7.0	-0.6	1.6	-1.2
Foreign exchange sales	5.2	2.0	2.7	6.6	9.0	3.7
Interest on money base	-0.5	-0.4	-0.6	-1.6	-0.3	-1.1

[a] Financial asset formation (including foreign currency-linked bank deposits), net of public credit to private sector.

Source: Annual Report 1985, Jerusalem: Bank of Israel, 1986.

improvement in the balance of payments in 1980 and 1984 was accompanied by accelerating inflation. Another approach was needed.

The policies introduced in 1981 were based on the theory that inflation was not related to real factors in the economy, such as the budget deficit, but was caused by the spiral of indexed wages, prices, and the exchange rate. The implication was that inflation had to be dealt with by "nominal" rather than "real" policy changes. These changes included the rate of devaluation and price rises; the latter was affected by the subsidy and indirect tax levels. If the government reduced the rate of increase in prices, inflationary expectations would be reduced, thus lowering future wage and price increases. In the past, inflation had been dealt with by managing the exchange rate, changing the prices of goods and services controlled by the government, and setting monetary targets. When balance-of-payments crises developed, the government devalued and increased the prices of controlled commodities. Its aim was to protect the foreign exchange reserves and implement a real devaluation. Indexation and a feeling that balance-of-payments problems were a more serious threat to the economy than inflation permitted the cost-push effect of the rise in controlled prices to increase the general level of prices. This price increase occurred within the context of accommodating monetary policy and was designed to protect the private sector from the effects of cuts in public sector expenditure. The underlying notion was that the problems in the economy stemmed from an excessive level of government spending.[11]

Some influential economists began to believe that an important link existed between the government deficit and the current account of the balance of payments. Excessive spending, financed by borrowing or printing money, increased the public's liquid assets. To protect the value of these assets against inflation and devaluation, the public bought foreign currency, thus worsening the balance of payments. This situation forced further devaluation, with the resulting inflation increasing government spending in nominal terms, borrowing and printing money, and so the spiral went on. The speed with which this inflationary spiral occurred was a function of the linkage system. A reduction of the budget deficit in the second half of 1985 made it much less necessary to sell foreign currency to the public, which, in turn, helped to bring about a commensurate improvement in the balance of payments.[12]

U.S. Influence

The United States took a much closer interest in Israeli economic policy beginning in 1984. Professor Stanley Fischer of the Massachusetts Institute of Technology, who had conducted research on the use of monetary policy in reducing inflation at the Bank of Israel, became adviser on Israeli economic affairs to the U.S. secretary of state. Professor Herbert Stein, also an economic adviser to the secretary of state, worked with Fischer on Israeli issues.

During 1985 a team of Israeli government officials and economists met with Fischer, Stein, and a group of U.S. government officials in connection with Israel's emergency economic program and increased U.S. assistance. They formed the Joint Economic Development Group, which was headed, on the Israeli side, by the director-general of the Ministry of Finance, Emmanuel Sharon. Other members included Professors Michael Bruno and Eitan Berglas; Amnon Neubach, economic adviser to the prime minister; and Mordecai Frenkel, head of the Bank of Israel's Research Department. The U.S. side was headed by Deputy Secretary of State Allan Wells; and it included Fischer, Stein, and representatives of the Pentagon, the State Department, and the U.S. Embassy in Israel.

The Americans advocated reductions in public expenditure, reduced government use of and control over the capital market, freezing the exchange rate, and lowering taxes. In this respect they were in general agreement with the consensus among Israeli economists, including many in the government.

The points made by Fischer in 1980, and later by Fischer and Stein, were developed in the Research Department of the Bank of Israel and in the Economics Department of Hebrew University. They were emphasized in a number of letters, made public, including one from the secretary of state to the Israeli prime minister in August 1986, and in a series of newspaper articles. They formed the basis of the economic stabilization program. The idea of publishing economic advice to the prime minister in the Israeli press may have originated in Israel: If the government was perceived by the public to be under pressure from the United States, then unpopular reforms might have been more acceptable.

Other Factors Behind Accelerating Inflation

Indexation of Assets

The system of indexation was a major cause of accelerating inflation. The linkage of government bonds and other assets to the foreign exchange rate, which began in 1977, reduced the length of lags in the system. Linkage to the consumer price index meant adjustment on a monthly basis, with a two-week lag: The increase in the index for any month was announced in the middle of the following month. Foreign exchange linkage increased liquidity because the exchange rate altered on a daily basis.[13]

Linkage of this kind prevented large shifts from financial to real assets. With the bulk of the public's savings linked, monetary accommodation to inflation was almost automatic. The government could not obtain resources from an inflation tax; in fact it lost them as a result of the inflation. (See "The Costs of Inflation" below.)

Daily changes in the exchange rate were a more important transmitter of inflation than monthly or quarterly linkage of wages. Government policies designed to reduce or contain real wages were apparently intended to reduce private consumption rather than to lower labor costs. As a result prices were increased in order to reduce purchasing power rather than relying on income tax changes and policies to control increases in wages and salaries.[14] The measures taken prior to July 1985 pushed up all costs.

The Income Tax System

The failure to fully link income tax brackets to increases in the cost of living meant that someone earning the average monthly salary of $500 in April 1985 paid nearly 30 percent in income tax and national and health insurance. Many professional workers contributed to educational and pension funds, which meant that net take-home pay came down to 65 percent of gross pay, or $325. High rates of income tax were felt to be a severe work disincentive. By January 1986 higher tax allowances and brackets increased take-home pay to 75.6 percent of gross pay. Income tax was back at levels similar to those that followed the 1975 reform in real terms. These calculations do not allow for a range of small benefits often paid to workers.

The failure to update tax brackets during the late 1970s and early 1980s reduced incentives to work overtime, thus reducing the extent to which capital equipment (often subsidized by the government) was used. It also encouraged more people to work in the black market economy, thus eroding the tax base and forcing the government to further increase the burden on those from whom tax was deducted at source. Proposals for a major tax reform, including lower tax rates and an ending of tax exemptions, were made in 1988 by a committee set up by the government. Two years later some, but not all, of its recommendations were implemented. If the report had been fully implemented, income tax levels would be similar, in real terms, to those that existed after the 1975 reform.

The Costs of Inflation

Inflation caused considerable damage to the economy in a number of ways. It affected the financial system as a whole and the planning system in companies. Worst of all it created massive uncertainties.

The Bank of Israel noted that hyperinflation made it difficult to determine a company's tax base. It eroded tax revenues because of the lag between the accrual of the tax liability and the payment of the tax. The tax base eroded despite larger deductions of taxes at source, tax advances from companies pegged to current turnover, monthly collections of value-added tax, and the linkage of local authority taxes to the consumer price index in 1985.

The lag between accrual and collection cost the Treasury at least $1 billion during 1984/85, 10 percent of the government's nominal revenue, when inflation was 15 percent a month. The lag in government payments for its outlays only partly compensated for this loss. The increase of inflation, from 9 to 13 percent a month during the period 1983–1984, caused an additional collection loss of $480 million, only partly compensated for by the erosion of tax brackets by $80 million. The temporary slowdown in inflation at the end of 1984 increased tax revenues by $180 million, and this situation occurred again after July 1985 with the introduction of the economic stabilization program.[15]

These were some of the direct losses to the government. Indirect losses included the need to continuously update budgets to cope with rising prices and wages, which occupied personnel in all sectors of the economy. The public was forced to spend a considerable amount of time at banks carrying out transactions in various consumer price index and foreign currency–linked assets in an effort to protect the value of its savings. The black market in foreign currency, principally the U.S. dollar, flourished as people tried to protect their savings against inflation.

The other side of this situation was an increase in the activities of the banks, the number of their personnel, and their purchases of equipment. In 1977, 25,700 people were employed by the banks; in 1983 this number had reached 37,554, an increase of 46 percent. These workers tended to be well educated, thus making them relatively expensive to employ. The banks made large investments in computerized equipment to cope with the ever rising number of transactions. These costs, designed to cope with inflation, have been estimated at 0.9 percent of GNP in 1978 and between 3.1 percent and 3.9 percent in 1982.[16] Inflation and the numbers employed by the banks rose in 1983 and so, therefore, did their costs. In 1984 prices rose sharply, but in the aftermath of the collapse of the bank shares in October 1983 (see Chapter 6), the banks' work force declined.

It was not only the banks that took on more workers to cope with the inflationary situation. Companies increased the number of employees dealing with cost accounting in an attempt to stay profitable in an increasingly difficult environment. This change did not cause an increase in industrial employment; it tended to shift managerial attention toward finance at the expense of production, marketing, and other productive functions, especially at the senior level.

A company selling $1 million worth of manufactured goods abroad would not know how many shekels it would get for the dollars when payment was made. The exchange rate was often adjusted by less than the inflation rate and so the value of the dollars earned could diminish. The cost of materials and labor also could not be predicted with inflation of up to 10 percent a month in 1982, 13 percent in 1983, 24 percent in 1984, and 27 percent in 1985. The costs of coping with this level of uncertainty were considerable and the economy is still recovering from it.

Inflation has persisted at an annual rate of about 20 percent since 1985, despite a serious recession between 1987 and 1989. The factors behind the persistence of inflation include the level of uncertainty about economic policy and the fact that the budget deficit has grown. The deficit is due to falling revenues, partly a function of the recession, and increased expenditure. The very uncompetitive nature of much of the economy is also an important cause of inflation: For many products there is no internal competition and for many others there is no competition from imports. Prices of services that are not traded internationally have risen as much as twice as fast as the overall increase in prices, an indication of the significance of competitive forces in those sectors where they exist. A shortage of housing, which is becoming more serious as thousands of immigrants arrive each month, is pushing up housing costs, an important component of the consumer price index.

Conclusion

Inflation at levels of over 100 percent a year was largely self-inflicted; it resulted mainly from economic mismanagement. The circumstances in which the economy found itself after the Yom Kippur War were extremely harsh, but it is significant that hyperinflation began in 1979 as the peace process with Egypt developed rather than during or just after the Yom Kippur War. Those were years of rising oil prices and a lack of consensus, even within the government, on economic policy. Behind these factors was a system of linkage, perfected by the introduction of foreign currency–linked assets. This transmitted inflation and inflationary expectations throughout the economy with great efficiency. The costs of hyperinflation were much greater than was realized at the time, and the costs incurred in bringing it to an end, in 1985, are still being felt in the 1990s.

Inflation continues at a rate that makes exports uncompetitive. There is, as a result, an expectation of devaluation nearly every six months, with all the uncertainty that entails. A further major reduction in inflation, which would remove the need for such frequent devaluations, will require structural changes aimed at increasing the level of competition in the economy.

Notes

1. *Annual Report 1974* (Jerusalem: Bank of Israel, 1975). In Hebrew.

2. M. Bruno, *External Shocks and Domestic Responses: Israel's Macro-Economic Performance 1965–1982,* in Y. Ben Porat, ed., *The Israeli Economy Through Crisis* (Cambridge, Mass.: Harvard University Press, 1986), p. 34.

3. *Recent Economic Developments* (Jerusalem: Bank of Israel, September 1985), no. 38, Table 16.

4. Ibid., Table 18, pp. 44–45.

5. D. Gottlieb and S. Piterman, "Inflationary Expectations in Israel," *Economic Review,* no. 57 (Jerusalem, 1985).

6. *The Budget 1986/87* (Jerusalem: Ministry of Finance, 1986). In Hebrew.

7. *Annual Report 1981* (Jerusalem: Bank of Israel, 1982).

8. *Annual Report 1982* (Jerusalem: Bank of Israel, 1983).

9. Z. Shiffer, "Money and Inflation in Israel: The Transition of an Economy to High Inflation," *Federal Reserve Board of St. Louis Review,* vol. 64 (St. Louis, August–September 1982), p. 33.

10. M. Bruno, "Economic Stabilization: The Emergency Plan in Its Early Phases," *Economic Quarterly,* vol. 31, no. 124 (Tel Aviv, October 1985). In Hebrew.

11. M. Bruno, *Israel's Stabilization: The End of the Lost Decade* (Jerusalem: Falk Institute, 1986).

12. N. Liviatan and S. Piterman, *Accelerating Inflation and Balance of Payments Crises. Israel 1973–84* (Jerusalem: Bank of Israel Discussion Paper Series, 1984).

13. E. Kleiman, *The Indexation of Public Sector Debt in Israel* (Jerusalem: Falk Institute, 1985).

14. Ibid.

15. Ibid.

16. E. Kleiman, "The Cost of Inflation," *Economic Quarterly,* vol. 119 (Tel Aviv, January 1984), in Hebrew, and *Annual Statistics of Israel's Banking System* (Jerusalem: Examiner of Banks, Bank of Israel, 1984 to 1987), in Hebrew.

3

Defense: Its Costs and Effects

The Composition and Growth of the Defense Budget

One of the most important elements of Israel's economic structure is the very high level of defense expenditure. Israel spends more per capita on defense than most Western countries and has done so for more than twenty years. In 1989 annual per capita expenditure was $1,402 in Israel, $1,166 in the United States, and $602 in the United Kingdom.[1] Defense expenditure equalled 15.2 percent of gross domestic product (GDP) in Israel, 5.6 percent in the United States, and 4.2 percent in the United Kingdom. This chapter examines the development of the defense sector and its role in the economy since the Yom Kippur War in 1973.

The Six-Day War of 1967 pushed up defense costs, as did the War of Attrition along the Suez Canal that followed it. Each war brought a rise in absolute levels of defense spending, and after the Yom Kipper War spending did not return to previous levels. The growing real cost of military equipment and the need to increase the size of the armed forces to match those of the Arab countries led to an increase in the burden of defense spending on the economy. A peak in budgeted defense expenditures was reached after the Yom Kippur War: Between 1973 and 1975 defense consumption equalled 32 percent of gross national product (GNP).[2] In 1990 defense expenditure funded by domestic sources (excluding U.S. military aid) was 57.8 percent higher in real terms than in 1970. During this period the GDP had, however, grown by only about 52 percent. The burden had, therefore, increased between 1970, a year of fighting along the Suez Canal, and 1990, a year in which the country saw relative peace along its borders, although the Palestinian uprising continued (see Table 3.1 and Figure 3.1).

The most important trend in the defense budget since 1967 has been the increased share spent on arms and military supplies purchased in the United States. These purchases have largely been financed by U.S. loans and grants.

TABLE 3.1
Index of Defense Expenditures, 1970 -1990
(1970 = 100)

Year	Total	Local [a]
1970	100.0	100.0
1971	99.7	114.5
1972	94.0	109.8
1973	154.8	141.6
1974	158.4	141.6
1975	177.6	164.0
1976	152.0	148.9
1977	122.2	172.3
1978	134.2	142.9
1979	115.8	145.5
1980	134.9	153.7
1981	148.0	157.2
1982	130.4	165.4
1983	121.6	166.4
1984	133.3	164.9
1985	143.3	160.8
1986	118.4	151.6
1987	155.1	154.8
1988	145.8	160.8
1989	118.7	157.8
1990	123.7	160.0

[a] Expenditure in the economy

Sources: 1970-1980: Calculated from: Supplement to the Monthly Bulletin of Statistics, Jerusalem: Central Bureau of Statistics, July 1984 Vol. 35, no. 7. 1981-1989: Calculated from: Supplement to the Monthly Bulletin of Statistics, Jerusalem: Central Bureau of Statistics, April 1990, Vol. 41, no. 5. 1990: Calculated from: Monthly Bulletin of Statistics, Jerusalem: Central Bureau of Statistics, January 1991, Vol. 42, no.1.

Figure 3.1 Index of Defense Expenditures, 1970-1990 (constant prices; 1970=100)

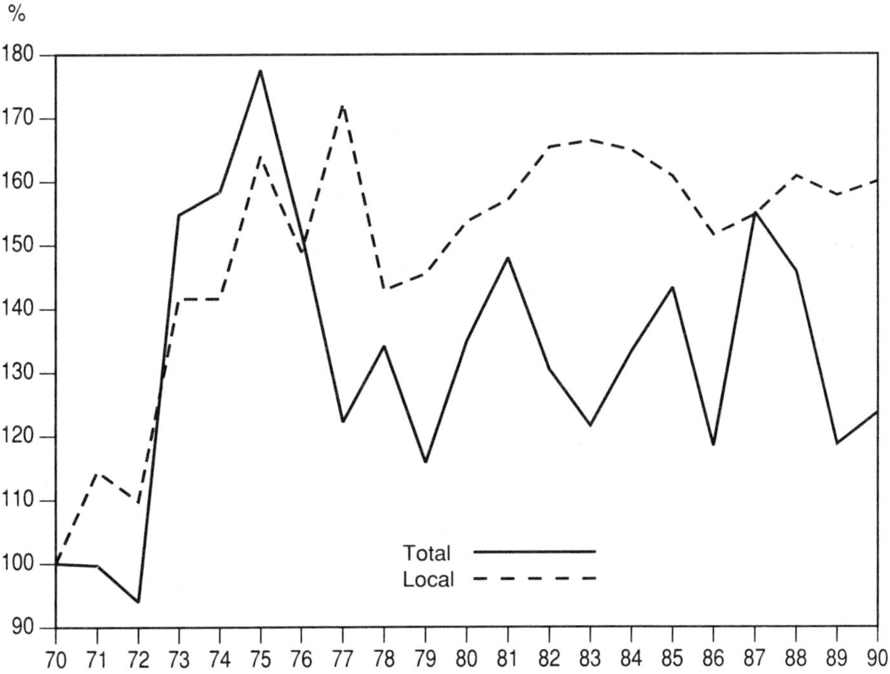

Source: Monthly Bulletin of Statistics, Central Bureau of Statistics

The next largest item consists of purchases of equipment from Israeli companies. In the mid-1980s these were also partly funded by the United States, mainly for the development of the Lavi fighter by Israel Aircraft Industries. Funds received by the Israeli government were exchanged for local currency, which was then used to pay domestic companies for work on the Lavi. The dollars were sold by the government to other sectors in the economy, thus reducing its need to raise revenues by other means.

Another large share of the budget covers salaries in the Ministry of Defense and the Israel Defense Forces (IDF), which employ about 3,000 civilians in various capacities who are paid salaries according to civil service wage scales. Approximately 170,000 permanent members of the armed forces are also paid a market wage.

The IDF comprises three elements. The conscript force is composed of 18- to 21-year-old men and 18- to 20-year-old women, who are paid a minimal salary. The permanent force consists mainly of officers who volunteer to serve in professional and fighting units. They are paid a market-related wage and receive full pensions upon reaching retirement, usually in their forties. There is a budget for pensions and compensation to retired and wounded soldiers and their families.

The 1991 defense budget totalled 14.3 billion shekels ($6.5 bn.), of which 9.3 bn. shekels are for local expenditure (which includes about $500 million of U.S. aid converted into local currency). U.S. military aid was forecast at $1.8 billion, and locally funded expenditure in foreign currency abroad, $150 million. (The 1991 budget was issued for the nine months from April to December 1991. The figures in the text have been annualized.)

Trends in Recent Years

Table 3.2 gives an indication of the burden of the defense budget and how it changed in the 1980s. Total defense expenditure, which includes defense imports, fluctuated widely each year because of the timing of major weapons systems deliveries. Year-to-year changes are not, therefore, an accurate guide as to how economic costs altered. Local defense expenditure excludes imports and has tended to be more stable than total defense expenditure. The table shows that the share of defense in GNP in the second half of the 1980s was lower than in the first half. In 1986 the burden was lowest according to three measures out of the four given in the table. The Palestinian uprising, which began at the end of 1987, did not result in a major increase in the burden but ended the trend toward lower defense expenditure. Most of the military cost of dealing with the uprising was accommodated within the defense budget. The increase in total military expenditure shown in Table 3.1 was the result of higher defense imports. Local expenditures remained stable and their share in national income has fallen (see Table 3.2).

Extrabudgetary Costs

There are large defense-related costs that are not covered by the defense budget; it is therefore necessary to include extrabudgetary items in a definition of the defense burden. The most important element of extrabudgetary costs has already been mentioned: The IDF does not pay the full cost of its use of conscripts and reservists. Conscripts, who are paid a nominal wage, bear the opportunity cost of their military service (their loss of income from alternative, civilian employment) almost completely; they do not receive a material reward for the service they provide to the country. Reservists do not receive their regular salaries while in uniform; rather they receive payments equal to their regular salary from national insurance funds to which they and their employers contribute.

TABLE 3.2
The Share of Budgeted Defense Expenditure in GNP, 1980-1990
(percent per annum)

	1980-1984[a]	1985	1986	1987	1988	1989	1990
Defense consumption as							
share of GNP and transfers	19.5	17.9	13.8	17.3	15.4	12.7	12.7
Total defense consumption minus grants	22.0	21.7	16.0	19.4	16.5	13.9	13.8
Domestic defense consumption [b]	14.3	12.7	11.0	10.8	10.6	10.4	10.1
Domestic and foreign funding [c]	18.1	17.7	15.1	14.4	13.8	13.2	12.5

[a] Annual average.
[b] Local currency expenditure net of defense sales.
[c] Includes budgeted foreign currency outlay, principal, and interest on U.S. government aid.

Sources: 1980-1984: Annual Report 1989, Jerusalem: Bank of Israel, 1990.
1985-1990: Annual Report 1990, Jerusalem: Bank of Israel, 1991.

The amount that each extra full-time soldier would produce if he or she left the army for civilian employment has been calculated in the following way. Labor's contribution to output is equal to 60 percent of the net product of taxes and subsidies. Calculating this amount on a national basis and then dividing it by the number of workers in the labor force gives an estimate of output per person of $10,000. This calculation assumes constant returns to scale: The addition of each worker (or indeed a whole demobilized army) to the labor force would not change economic conditions so as to alter the estimate of output per person. In reality, any addition to the labor force changes economic conditions and a substantial demobilization would have significant effects that cannot be estimated here. Assuming that reservists serve an average of one month per year, the annual cost comes to between $308 million and $370 million, or between 1.2 percent and 1.5 percent of national income.[3]

In 1988, according to the International Institute for Strategic Studies, Israel had 110,000 conscripts.[4] The only way that their cost to the economy can be estimated is to assume that out of uniform the conscript would produce some level of output. This amount may relate to the average level of output per capita in the economy if there is no unemployment but is unlikely to equal it because 18- to 21-year-olds do not have the training and experience of the average worker. In conditions of unemployment their potential output will be lower; as of the early 1990s, several thousand discharged solders are unemployed.

Although the cost of conscription to the economy is considerable, reducing the size of the army would, at least in the short term, present serious problems. The Israeli economy, with a total labor force of about 1.5 million, would find it extremely difficult to absorb an increase in the labor supply of 6.5 percent represented by the demobilization of 110,000 conscripts at once. This condition would be true even in an environment of lower defense spending, which might make more resources available for the generation of alternative employment. The question is therefore one of time scale: Over time the adjustment would be easier; the economy could adjust to a series of incremental changes more easily than to a single large adjustment. The longer the period over which demobilization occurs, the lower the adjustment cost.

Making assumptions of this kind is the only way in which the cost of conscription can be estimated. Allowing for the lower potential productivity of conscripts relative to the average worker leads to an estimated output loss of between $5,000 and $6,000 per conscript per year. The total annual cost is therefore between $550 and $600 m. ($5,500–$6,000 multiplied by 110,000 conscripts), or about 2 percent of GNP.

Another extrabudgetary cost is that of pensions: Government employees do not make contributions during their working lives to official pension funds; this situation applies to both civilian employees of the Ministry of Defense and career soldiers. These costs have been estimated at between 1 and 2 percent of GNP. Further, the stockpiling of fuel and other essential commodities for military purposes may cost the equivalent of 0.5 percent of GNP. Facilities for stockpiling have to be built, maintained, and guarded. The funds used to buy fuel and other stockpiled items could otherwise earn foreign currency. Civil defense in terms of building shelters alone may cost another 0.5 percent of GNP.[5] Total extrabudgetary costs calculated here, therefore, come to about 6 percent of GNP.

Other costs are incurred by central and local governments under different budget headings. The defense establishment owns land in the center of the country for which it does not pay rent; the rent that these parcels of land could yield from other uses is also lost and is another implicit economic cost.

Another incalculable cost is that of disruption of the labor force; although this disruption is most obvious during periods of war, it also occurs in peacetime. The mobilization of reservists each year means that workers are unable to report for work. The real loss of output not only is what they would have produced had they remained at work but also includes the cost of disruption caused by their absence. One person's absence affects the output of other workers. Managers have to double or triple their responsibilities when their colleagues go on reserve duty, with negative consequences for efficiency and production.

Reservists are usually notified when and for how long they must serve, but mobilization exercises are also conducted to test the efficiency of the system, and these tests cause unplanned disruptions. By their very nature these costs cannot be calculated. They have to be met in normal conditions; when war breaks out there are additional costs.

The Cost of War

The cost of Israel's military involvement in Lebanon between 1982 and 1985 has been estimated at $5 billion.[6] This estimate includes additions to the national debt caused by the war and the cost of Israel's military buildup to keep pace with the Syrian army, which followed the period of most severe fighting in 1982.

Israel's net foreign liabilities at the end of 1980 were $12 billion; by the end of 1985, the year most Israeli forces left Lebanon, they had reached $19.1 billion. Net interest payments abroad rose from $600 million in 1979 to $1.0 billion in 1982 and $1.7 billion in 1984.[7] Not all of the increase was caused by the war; changes in economic policy that increased private consumption, during 1981, also led to a rise in the foreign debt.

Other costs of war include increased reserve duty, losses of military equipment and fuel, losses of industrial and other output, reduced tourism, and, of course, increased casualties. An immeasurable cost of the war in Lebanon was the considerable damage to military and national morale, which may have resulted, inter alia, in more emigration and less immigration. It is not known over how long a period the $5 billion cost will be incurred: Some costs, such as purchases of equipment, are immediate, while others, including the effect of higher taxation on work incentives, investment, and civilian output, will be carried into the future. In 1982, the Bank of Israel noted in its *Annual Report* that spreading the cost of replenishing military supplies and equipment over several years would lighten the economic burden in 1982 but would prolong it thereafter, thus impeding economic growth and making budget cuts more difficult.[8]

One of the most serious repercussions of high and fluctuating military expenditures is the rapid rate of change and uncertainty that they produce in important sectors of the economy. The largest fluctuations in recent years have been in the construction sector, associated with the withdrawal of the IDF from Sinai following the peace treaty with Egypt. In 1980, for example, domestic purchases from the construction sector rose by 52 percent. This situation necessitated importing workers from abroad to avoid causing shortages in the local industry and thus promoting inflationary pressures.

Fluctuations in purchases of goods and services from the defense budget in areas other than construction are much more significant because of the size of these items in the budget. The implications for the economy are examined in "Military Industries" and "Market Structure of the Defense Industry" below.

Reserve duty increased when the Palestinian uprising broke out in 1987 and continues at a higher level than previously. Between 1988 and 1991 about $500 million was allocated, mainly within the defense budget, to cover the military costs of the uprising.[9] This situation has also increased the extrabudgetary burden of defense.

The Iraqi invasion of Kuwait in August 1990 and the Gulf War in January–March 1991 resulted in losses of approximately $3 billion in the Israeli economy. Tourist revenues fell by $500 million, and imports of oil cost $400 million more than in the corresponding period of 1989–1990. There was a loss of output worth $1.1 billion when the missile attacks on Israel brought the economy to a temporary standstill. Direct damage from the missile attacks is estimated at $60 million and budgetary costs (mainly due to increased military activity) came to $750 million. Balance-of-payments costs—loss of export earnings and higher interest charges—equalled about $250 million.[10]

TABLE 3.3
Civilian, Military Aid, and Defense Imports, 1980-1990
(current dollars, millions)

	1980	1985	1989	1990
1. Grants	1556	3885	2769	3253
2. Loans	1368	0	0	0
3. Loan repayment	563[a]	1055	1826	1088
Principal	215	109	987	231
Interest	363	946	839	857
4. Gross total (1+2)	2924	3885	2769	3253
5. Net total (4 minus 3)	2361	2830	943	2165
6. Defense imports	1655	1792	1225	1500

[a] Principal and interest do not add up to total in source.

Sources: 1980: Annual Report 1984, Jerusalem: Bank of Israel, 1985.
1985 and 1989: Annual Report 1989, Jerusalem: Bank of Israel, 1990.
1990: Annual Report, Jerusalem: Bank of Israel, 1991.

Foreign Aid and Other Resources: The U.S. Connection

As an indicator of the defense burden, the calculation of defense costs as a share of GNP is somewhat misleading because Israel has access to resources in excess of its national income. These additional resources include U.S. loans and grants, details of which are given in Table 3.3. An accurate definition of available resources would also include a deduction for debt repayment. A serious complication is the need to calculate what sum to consider as a result of the military threat to Israel. Economic assistance from the United States and Jewish communities outside Israel is closely related to Israel's strategic position: At times of threat, U.S. assistance has increased.

In 1980, loans from the U.S. government equalled 7.1 percent of GNP; grants came to 7.4 percent. Other loans and transfers equalled 9.4 percent; the total inflow of resources from abroad was equivalent to 23.9 percent of GNP. Total resources, which are defined as GNP plus inflows from abroad, therefore, came to 123.9 percent of GNP. Net total resources are defined as GNP plus the inflow of aid and loans minus debt repayments.

Debt repayments were equal to 9 percent of GNP and so net total resources came to 114.9 percent of GNP.

The simple definition of the defense burden is the share of defense expenditure in GNP; in 1980 this share came to 25.2 percent. After military aid is deducted, the domestic defense burden is 15 percent. Adding extrabudgetary costs to this amount provides a more refined calculation, equal to 24.8 percent of GNP or 21.6 percent of net total resources.[11] Some of the calculations for 1989 are given in Table 3.2. Adding 6 percent for extrabudgetary items gives a ratio of defense consumption to GNP plus transfers of 18.7 percent.

Apart from military assistance, the United States provides Israel with civilian aid. Contributions from the world Jewish community have also been of considerable importance as a source of foreign exchange and have been used to help defray the costs of social and educational programs. Donations totalled $868 million in 1989 and $1.2 billion in 1990.

Table 3.3 shows how U.S. assistance has helped to meet the immediate costs of defense imports but has also increased the debt burden. A number of significant trends are apparent. Between 1980 and 1989 the volume of loans fell sharply, while that of grants increased by 78 percent. Loan repayments more than quadrupled and the burden of interest payments more than doubled. Gross aid, in current dollars, declined by 5 percent between 1980 and 1989, while net aid (aid received less repayment) fell by 60 percent. In real terms, the value of aid declined continuously. These figures include civilian aid, which increased by $750 million in 1986 and 1987 as a result of an emergency assistance package granted in connection with the July 1985 economic stabilization program. In 1990, to help overcome costs resulting from the Gulf War, the United States provided Israel with $750 million of military assistance.

Military Industries

The defense effort has had major ramifications throughout Israeli society, economy, and industry. It has affected attitudes and motivation as well as institutions and development.

There is no clear definition of what constitutes the defense sector because few companies manufacture solely for the IDF and foreign military markets; most companies produce a mix of military and civilian goods. It has been estimated that between 58,000 and 120,000 people work in military industries, depending on the definition used.[12] The lower estimate is equal to 20 percent of the industrial work force and to between 4 percent and 5 percent of the total labor force, including up to 50 percent of Israel's scientists and engineers.[13] The *1987/88 Israel Defense Sales Directory* advertised 180 companies, an indication of the size of the sector.

TABLE 3.4
Exports of Sectors Most Closely Associated with Defense, 1980-1990
(current dollars, millions)

Year	Electronic and Electric	Transport Equipment	Machinery	Total
1980	263	372	171	806
1985	776	420	136	1,332
1990	1,634	581	317	2,532

Sources: 1980 and 1985: Foreign Trade Statistics Quarterly; Vol.39, no. 4, (October-December 1988), Jerusalem: Central Bureau of Statistics, March 1989; 1990: Foreign Trade Statistics Quarterly, Vol 41, no. 4 (October-December 1990), Jerusalem: Central Bureau of Statistics, March 1991.

Israel Aircraft Industries (IAI), Israel's largest industrial company, is also its major defense producer. Its 1990 sales were $1.4 billion, of which $1.1 billion was exported.[14]

The total output of the metals, machinery, electronics, and electrical goods sectors in 1989 has been estimated at about $7.5 billion, or about 19 percent of GNP.[15] This figure includes civilian sales and is, therefore, biased upward as an estimate of the output of military industries. It is, however, an indication of the size of a sector in which nonmarket considerations play an important role. Table 3.4 gives an indication of the growth of exports in these sectors.

Although the origins of military industries predate the state, a major impetus for the development of more sophisticated production came in the late 1960s. In 1967, France, then Israel's major arms supplier, declared an embargo on arms supplies to Israel. To overcome the large gap caused by the embargo, Israel decided to increase local production and purchase equipment from the United States on a much greater scale.

The Ministry of Defense has had a strong industrial policy. Its role in the development of industry dates back to an earlier period. In 1948 it set up Rafael, the Armament Development Authority, as a department of the ministry. In 1959–1960, Rafael became a civilian authority producing and advising on weapons systems for the IDF, employing 6,500, including 2,500 in research and development. A separate organization, Israel Military Industries, operates as part of the Ministry of Defense.

Research, development, and production of a wide range of industrial products started after the 1967 war, and with spin-offs in civilian product areas, industrial production grew rapidly. The IDF provided a large market for these products and was able to impose high standards and test products. Its use of these items in war became an important sales feature in export markets. An example was the decision by a foreign customer to purchase whichever of the two Israeli-produced drones (unmanned mini-aircraft) that the IDF decided to purchase.[16]

In 1961 the ministry pushed for the merger of two companies, Tadir and Ran, to form Tadiran, jointly owned by the government and Koor, the industrial conglomerate belonging to the Histadrut national labor federation. Tadir was a producer of communications equipment and Ran produced military and civilian batteries. The government sold 50 percent of Tadiran's equity to General Telephone and Electric (GTE) of the United States in order to acquire U.S. technology, management, and marketing expertise. In 1983 GTE sold its share to Koor. Tadiran's 1980 sales were $280 million; in 1990 they were $800 million, making it Israel's second largest manufacturing company.

In 1985 Tadiran recorded a 40 percent fall in profits and a sales growth rate of only 3 percent, largely because of a fall in the volume of orders from the Ministry of Defense. Firms in the defense sector have a limited ability to substitute export or civilian orders for domestic military ones because of the lead time needed for such sales. Given the large number of companies involved in defense production, this is a considerable problem in the Israeli economy. Civilian exports are increasing; they constitute over half of the exports of the electronics sector.

Israel Aircraft Industries was founded as a maintenance base for the Israel Airforce and El Al Israel Airlines. In 1988 it employed 16,500 people.[17] In the 1970s Israel Aircraft Industries began to design, develop, and later produce prototypes of its own fighter aircraft, the Lavi. From its very inception the project was the subject of controversy. Production costs were estimated at over $2 billion and Israel temporarily joined the very small group of countries individually developing and producing fighter aircraft.[18] In concentrating resources on the Lavi, Israel followed a pattern observed in the United States: a tendency to concentrate on a small number of large projects with rapidly escalating costs.[19] This practice further reinforced the trend toward inflexibility in production. The United States, which had been funding part of the program, exerted strong pressure for its cancellation. The Lavi was scrapped after a long and heated public debate; $500 million was allocated for severance pay and other costs and $350 million for alternative projects.[20]

The government also owns Israel Shipyards, which manufactures exclusively for the Navy and has recently been on the verge of closure. Bet Shemesh Engines was founded at the end of the 1960s as a partnership with a French jet engine manufacturer; its future has been uncertain for years and it has hardly made a profit since it was founded.

There are also a large number of private companies involved in military production that have grown in close cooperation with the Ministry of Defense. Perhaps the most important example of private sector activity in this field is the Discount Investment Company (DIC), Israel's largest private holding company. It was founded in 1961 by the Discount Banking Group, with a former commander of the Israel Airforce, Dan Tolkovsky, as its managing director and vice-chairman. In the 1960s Tolkovsky identified the need for Israel to develop a high-technology industrial base for military as well as economic reasons. DIC was instrumental in setting up Elron Electronic Industries, Ltd., an industrial holding group with subsidiaries and affiliates involved in the development, manufacture, and marketing of a range of industrial goods.

The military sector has certain inherent advantages that have benefitted the economy. Companies concentrating on military production tend to have relatively good industrial relations, partly because they employ skilled and therefore well-paid workers. Employees are conscious of their centrality to the national defense effort, a motivational factor of considerable importance. These firms are also capital intensive and are technologically very sophisticated. They usually have a high degree of product concentration with only limited competition, but this is not always the case: Intense competition at home and abroad between Israel Aircraft Industries and Tadiran for sales of drones, for example, eventually resulted in the formation of a joint company.

Military products produced in Israel are not guaranteed a market in the IDF. The defense establishment policy has generally been to supply the IDF with the best equipment, not necessarily that made at home. Domestic production, therefore, has to compete with imports. The IDF has an incentive to buy abroad when imports are cheaper (given that quality considerations do not outweigh cost), but decisions are also influenced by the desire to provide orders to local producers so as to maintain domestic production capabilities.[21] Cuts in the domestically funded defense budget have led to pressures in the military establishment to buy more basic goods, such as uniforms, abroad. The budget funded by U.S. aid has been large enough to cover the cost of more sophisticated purchases, leaving room for basic items.

Many other countries prefer to manufacture their own arms where possible rather than to rely on imports; they are, therefore, of limited value as markets. As many countries do not maintain diplomatic relations with Israel or are subject to pressure from Arab countries, some arms sales have been blocked. The dangers of reliance on arms exports are considerable.

The 10 percent real reduction in local purchases between 1984 and 1986 by the Ministry of Defense resulted in a contraction of the market for Israeli producers. Total defense spending fell less than domestic spending because of increased U.S. assistance. However, most of the funds provided by the United States are tied to purchases of goods made there. The definition of "made in America" is that at least 51 percent of the product should be made in the United States. In order to meet the U.S. requirement, a number of Israeli companies set up production facilities in the United States so that the U.S. facilities can produce at least 51 percent of the orders financed by U.S. aid. At least seven Israeli companies were manufacturing in the United States in 1985 for this purpose.[22]

Market Structure of the Defense Industry

The importance of the structure of an industry as a determinant of its behavior and growth has been emphasized by a number of economists.[23] The less competitive the industry and its market is, the lower its growth. If the industry is large and uncompetitive, its effect on the economy will be to reduce the rate of growth of GNP.

The conditions in an optimal, free-market situation have been contrasted with those that prevail in the U.S. defense market. A brief examination of the U.S. position reveals significant Israeli parallels.

Among the main characteristics of free markets are the large number of small producers and consumers, none of whom can have a significant effect on the market. Commodities traded are small and divisible, and prices are determined by competition in the market and respond to changes in supply and demand. There is mobility of factors of production, perfect information (everyone in the market has all the information needed to make decisions), free movement in and out of markets.

The U.S. defense market is characterized by monopsony (a monopolistic purchaser), oligopoly, and the indivisibility of products. Prices are determined in relation to total costs and military need (on a cost-plus basis): Weapons systems take years to develop; capital and labor are not mobile, and the government intervenes as regulator, specifier, banker, and judge of claims. Finally, competition is for all or none of a market rather than for shares of it. Barriers to entry include the fact that sales are made to the government through close contact with its purchasing officers. Winning government contracts is a specialized, complex task. Although capital investment needed for defense production may be high, the market is limited to what the defense budget allows plus any possible exports. Lowering prices may not affect sales if military needs have been met, something even more true of Israel than the United States. There are close links between the defense establishment and supplying companies that involve the interchange of personnel.

Price is less important than performance: Firms cannot reduce unit costs by duplicating existing products at lower prices because markets are limited. The pressure is usually to improve performance. Research and development are the keys to product improvement and new systems, but they are expensive activities. The costs involved may not be feasible. Defense ministries may lend equipment to firms in the industry as part of joint projects but may be less willing to do so with new entrants whom they know less well. Given the tendency toward large projects, the size of the investments required may be prohibitive. The defense establishment may demand particular reporting, accounting, management, and other technical systems that are unique to the defense sector and require knowledge before they can be adopted.[24]

There are also factors that prevent or discourage companies from leaving the industry. Defense contracts may encourage financially weak companies to stay in the market rather than seek capital from other sources. Government funding provides an incentive to remain in the hope of making a civilian commercial application as well as military ones. Equipment required for defense production often cannot be converted for use in manufacturing civilian goods. The ability of specially trained personnel to move into civilian production may be limited. For example, defense industry marketing skills are different from civilian ones, and the cost pressures prevailing in civilian markets may be difficult for firms used to operating in a cost-plus environment. Given the increasingly long-term nature of military product development, diversification may take years to plan. Local companies may not want to abandon the market to foreign suppliers, nor may governments want them to.[25]

Israel's defense industry has many of these characteristics. The defense sector is only partly subject to competitive pressures; its importance in the economy means that this uncompetitiveness exerts a significant influence on the system as a whole. Its civilian markets are too small for economies of scale to be achieved in domestic production as often as economies of scale are achieved in larger economies. Monopoly and oligopoly are widespread, and prices are often either controlled by the government or strongly influenced by it. Capital is immobile because the state dominates the capital market, and labor mobility is limited by trade union and other agreements.

Defense and Its Prominence in Decision Making

Israel is unique in having been founded in war and having remained so ever since. Few countries have been subject to so much active and passive hostility by so many and for so long. Defense has almost always come first in terms of the overall allocation of resources. Great efforts have been made by the political leadership to obtain financial and technological resources for the IDF and military industries.

The centrality of the defense effort in Israeli life has been described in the following terms:

> The control of the execution of centralized policies and decisions is performed through the Israeli social structure, where managers are much better acquainted with each other than they are in countries with populations similar to that of Israel. This is true mainly because of Israel's geo-political position, its relatively isolated and self-centered economy and its business managers being associated with each other in different social systems, primarily in their service in the IDF's reserves.[26]

The IDF is an important socializing agent in Israeli society; it also provides many with a common motivation. Although the consensus on political and economic issues has declined in recent years, the army still plays a unifying social role.[27]

The size of the IDF and the industrial complex with which it is associated has been one reason why the government has played an important role in the economy since independence. Defense industries have either been run by the government directly or, often, by former army officers or reservists whose outlook, ideology, and motivation were affected by their army service. The size and preponderance of the military sector also mean that many of the decisions in the economy are made as a result of military rather than economic considerations or, at most, with economic factors being only one of the deciding criteria. Many important decisions affecting the economy are made within the confines of the defense establishment with minimal external influence.

In recent years, defense has had a reduced priority. The domestic consensus about the nation's political-military aims has weakened. This change resulted from controversy about the settlement program in the West Bank and Gaza as well as from intense dissatisfaction with the conduct of the war in Lebanon. The peace treaty with Egypt and the Iran-Iraq war made many, including the General Staff, feel that Israel was in a relatively strong position in the region. During 1988 this belief began to change with the end of the Iran-Iraq war and the continuation of the Palestinian uprising in the West Bank and Gaza. This change in belief may have been reinforced by missile attacks on Israel during the 1991 Gulf War.

The deteriorating performance of the economy made the allocation of resources for defense more difficult. Social services were cut to a point where the opportunity cost of defense spending became clearer to the public and the government. This action was a factor behind the cancellation of the Lavi.

Conclusion: Defense and Economic Growth

Military necessity has forced the government to play a major role in the economy. From 1948 until 1977 the country was ruled by a social democratic party that believed in government intervention in the context of a mixed economy. A key question is whether Israel's economy would have developed in a different way without government intervention through the defense effort.

The ideas put forward by Gerschenkron suggest that countries trying to develop in the mid-twentieth century cannot succeed without government intervention.[28] Germany in the latter part of the nineteenth century had to involve the banks in the development of industry in a way that had not been necessary half a century before in the United Kingdom. Germany also had to compete with the already industrialized United Kingdom and so needed a different development mechanism. Russia, before the revolution, experienced massive state investment in basic industries, which had not happened in the United Kingdom or Germany. Postwar Japan developed on the basis of very close links between the government and industrial conglomerates. Against this background, the development of military industries can be seen as a means by which the Israeli government was able to push economic development forward. However, since 1973 Israel's large-scale military spending has been accompanied by economic stagnation, and some commentators have suggested that the government has gone too far, from an economic point of view, in developing military production.[29]

The most superficial statistical investigation bears this assertion out. As the defense burden has grown, so the rate of economic growth has fallen. In the 1980s the defense burden stabilized and then fell slightly, but it remained at a very high absolute level. After allowing for the fact that inputs of labor and capital grew more slowly in recent years, this correlation between high levels of defense expenditure and slow economic growth suggests that there is a threshold beyond which defense spending does have a negative effect. The nature and existence of such a threshold is a matter for further research.

Foreign aid has accounted for an increasing share of the defense budget and this situation has caused the ratio of defense expenditure to GNP to be biased upward. It has been shown, however, that after allowing for debt repayment for military borrowing the true ratio was not lower. Extrabudgetary costs need to be added to the calculation.

Showing a correlation between high defense/GNP ratios and slow GNP growth does not mean that the former is the cause of the latter. There is, however, a priori evidence for such a conclusion: The output of the defense sector does not yield economic benefits; it is not meant to.

If it is assumed that the whole of the metals, electronics, and electrical sectors was the result of military-inspired government intervention, then their contribution to the economy can be set off against the costs of defense. One measure of their contribution is exports. In 1985 they equalled about 6 percent of GNP compared to direct defense imports of 7.6 percent. What cannot easily be calculated is what the level of exports would have been in a low defense spending situation and precisely what the level of indirect defense imports was. Finally, for a complete picture, it would be necessary to calculate the level of civilian imports required by the reduced level of domestic production.

Had the government decided not to set up military industries and stimulate arms production, it could still have pushed economic development in other ways. The alternatives were not "defense" and "no growth." The government could have found ways to stimulate civilian output through either the public sector or the private sector or both. Arms imports might have been higher but exports might have more than compensated for them.

The trade-off between economic growth and defense spending is complex. If growth is assumed to be synonymous with increased exports, then in any one year there is a trade-off between allocations for exports and those for defense. The government can spend money on one or the other. In addition, allocations for domestic expenditure stimulate local demand, thus increasing imports and at the same time reducing the room for and incentive to export.

Promotion of exports may, therefore, be at the expense of defense consumption, which yields noneconomic benefits in the short term, or defense investment, which yields noneconomic benefits in the future. However, allocations for defense at the expense of export development reduce the size of future GNP and thus the economy's ability to fund future defense spending.[30] Civilian investment can be substituted for export allocations in this argument.

As a result of Israel's political and military situation, the country developed a very close relationship with the United States, which resulted in flows of aid and military hardware, accompanied by significant effects on the economy. As of the early 1990s, the prospects for aid continuing at levels that prevailed in the 1980s are fading. The need for reform in the domestic economy, designed to increase self-sufficiency, is increasing, and the role of foreign aid in reducing pressures for reform is clear.

There is no consensus in economic literature on the effects of defense expenditure on economic growth and development, but Israel's current experience leads to certain conclusions. The defense buildup led to major industrial development, but the costs of military spending increased the size of the state budget, the budget deficit, and inflationary finance. These were important factors behind the acceleration of inflation and the slowdown of economic growth. Israel's move into high-technology military production resulted in slower growth of civilian output than otherwise would have occurred. Traditional industries were upgraded at a slower rate, and as a result they were left behind technologically and denied skilled manpower. Shifting 1,000 technologically trained personnel from military to civilian research and development could have, according to one estimate made in the mid-1980s, increased GNP growth by 1 percent.[31] Even if these estimates of the costs are overstated, the effect is considerable. This effect, combined with the burdens described above, amounts to a considerable economic loss.

Notes

1. *The Military Balance 1989/90* (London: International Institute for Strategic Studies, 1989).
2. *Annual Report 1984* (Jerusalem: Bank of Israel, 1985). In Hebrew.
3. H. Barkai, "Reflections on the Economic Cost of the Lebanon War," *Jerusalem Quarterly*, no. 37 (Jerusalem, 1986).
4. *The Military Balance 1988/89* (London: International Institute for Strategic Studies, 1988).
5. E. Berglas, *Defense and the Economy: The Israeli Experience* (Jerusalem: Falk Institute for Economic Research in Israel, 1983).
6. Barkai, "Reflections on the Economic Cost of the Lebanon War."
7. *Annual Report 1984* (Jerusalem: Bank of Israel, 1985). In Hebrew.
8. *Annual Report 1982* (Jerusalem: Bank of Israel, 1983). In Hebrew.
9. *Main Points of the Budget 1991* (Jerusalem: Ministry of Finance, 1990). In Hebrew.
10. Ministry of Finance figures quoted on Israel Television, 23 April 1991.
11. P. Rivlin, "The Burden of Defense: The Case of Israel," in *World Armaments and Disarmament SIPRI Yearbook 1983* (Stockholm: Stockholm International Peace Research Institute, 1983).
12. A. Klieman, *Israel's Global Reach* (London: Pergamon Brassey's, 1985), p. 57.
13. Ibid.
14. *Ha'aretz* (Tel Aviv), 16 April 1991. In Hebrew.
15. *Ministry of Industry and Trade, Budget 1990* (Jerusalem: Ministry of Finance, 1990).
16. *Report of the State Comptroller 1984*, no. 35 (Jerusalem: State Comptroller's Office, 1984). In Hebrew.

17. *Report and Accounts of Government Companies to March 1989* (Jerusalem: Ministry of Finance, Government Companies Authority, 1989). In Hebrew.

18. Y. Peri and A. Neubach, *The Military Industrial Complex in Israel: A Pilot Study* (Tel Aviv: International Center for Peace in the Middle East, January 1985).

19. J. Gansler, *The Defense Industry* (Cambridge, Mass.: MIT Press, 1980), p. 16.

20. *Davar*, 8 March 1987. In Hebrew.

21. Peri and Neubach, *The Military Industrial Complex in Israel.*

22. *Ma'ariv* (Tel Aviv), 2 August 1985. In Hebrew.

23. M. Porter, *Competitive Strategy: Techniques for Analyzing Industries and Competitors* (New York: Free Press, 1980), and Gansler, *The Defense Industry.*

24. Gansler, *The Defense Industry.*

25. Ibid.

26. T. Weinshall, *Decision Making in Top Management Teams of Israeli Organizations* (Tel Aviv: Tel Aviv University, Faculty of Management Working Paper, no. 615/79, July 1979).

27. M. Radom, "Military Officers and Business Leaders: An Israeli Study in Contrasts," *Columbia Journal of World Business* (New York, March/April 1968).

28. A. Gerschenkron, *Economic Backwardness in Historical Perspective* (Cambridge, Mass.: Harvard University Press, 1962).

29. Peri and Neubach, *The Military Industrial Complex in Israel.*

30. A. Halperin, *Military Build-up and Economic Growth in Israel* (Jerusalem: Maurice Falk Institute Conference Paper, June 1986).

31. Ibid.

4

Industry and Agriculture

In 1990, industry produced 20.4 percent of gross domestic product (GDP). Agriculture accounted for 5.8 percent. More of the output of these sectors has been exported, or has the potential for export, than that of other sectors (with the exception of tourism). Their role in the economy and the trend toward increasing foreign trade are therefore crucial. In 1990 they accounted for 29.6 percent and 8.5 percent, respectively, of the business sector's GDP. The rest of the business sector during this period consisted of transport and communications (15.2 percent), power and water (3.9 percent), and building (9.8 percent), little of which is internationally traded. Services and trade accounted for 33.0 percent.

Industrial Policy Development

A review of the development of industrial policy provides an important focus on the problems currently facing the economy and industry in particular. It also shows how important the government has been in the development of the economy and why there are still conflicts over the extent of the government's economic activities.

The 1940s and 1950s

In the industrial structure Israel inherited from the British mandate the supply of locally made consumer goods was greater than that of investment goods. After 1948 economic policy attempted to deepen the industrial structure by creating industries that would provide the inputs needed by other sectors. In the 1950s the government also aimed to expand employment for the large number of immigrants arriving in the country and to supply basic commodities to the local market. These goals were achieved through import substitution (encouraging domestic production by preventing imports from coming into the country) in order to make the economy more self-sufficient and because there were serious shortages of foreign exchange. Industries were set up throughout the country with government assistance in the form of subsidies, loans, and loan guarantees. The government also undertook the task of raising funds abroad to finance investment.

Despite the degree of control exercised by the central government, there was no effective overall planning of the economy. The first plan drawn up for the period 1950–1953 was not implemented because government ministries were unwilling to give up some of their powers. The economy was always conceived as mixed, with a private as well as a public sector. There was never the commitment to strong planning that existed in the Soviet Union, for example. This situation has been the case throughout Israel's history; the government has played a central role in the economy but has not acted according to a master plan or even a clear set of principles. There remains a lack of coordination between ministries and official bodies, and no government has been able to push through long-term reforms.

Within this framework emphasis was placed during the early years of the state on the development of the resources of the Negev. This emphasis led to the foundation of the chemical and fertilizer sectors, based on the Dead Sea potash and phosphates extraction industries. The government was also involved in the development of a wide range of other industries. Government-owned or -controlled companies in 1952 included El Al Israel Airlines, Arkia domestic airlines, Bedek Aircraft Maintenance (forerunner of Israel Aircraft Industries), Ran Batteries, the Chemicals and Phosphates Company, the Dead Sea Works, the Israel Water Planning Company, and the Jerusalem Economic Corporation, which was responsible for assisting industrial development in the capital. In addition the government was involved in the management of at least twenty-seven other firms. In 1954 the state also bought 54 percent of the shares of the Electric Corporation, which had been founded in 1923.

As stated in Chapter 1, there was an emphasis on agricultural investment at the expense of industry. In the late 1950s industrial policy continued to focus on generating employment on the basis of import substitution in industry. Private sector investment in industry was much larger than in agriculture, but the role of the state was greater than the figures indicate because it controlled bank and other credit lines, thus wielding major influence on the scale and pattern of investment throughout the economy.

In 1954 the government established the Investment Center and in 1959 the Investment Authority. In an effort to encourage foreign investment, the Law for the Encouragement of Capital Investment was passed by the Knesset in 1954. It provided the legal framework for subsidized loans for capital investments by companies with Investment Center approval. It remains one of the centerpieces of government support for industry. Some of the major companies in Israel today were founded with investment assistance given under this law.

The initial purpose of the Investment Center and the Investment Authority was to channel funds donated by philanthropists into productive investment. Later they became involved in promoting investment in Israel. The Industrial Development Bank was founded in 1958 with funds provided by the government to make loans to industry in accordance with official priorities. Interest rates had virtually no role in investment allocation and were set at low levels. Furthermore, as Halevi and Klinov-Malul state, there was no clear connection between rates of return and trends in investment.[1]

The marginal productivity, or efficiency, of an investment was, therefore, determined bureaucratically on the basis of government decisions rather than by market forces. Subsidized interest rates and the lack of full linkage to the consumer price index or the dollar exchange rate of the sum to be repaid resulted in unnecessarily high capital intensity in many sectors. As a result, the growth of employment was limited, and industrial capacity was not utilized efficiently.

In the 1950s the emphasis on economic self-sufficiency meant that industrial exports were not considered a priority. Production was carried out to meet the requirements of the domestic markets, and goods that could not be sold at home were, where possible, sold abroad. Foreign sales were often done on a barter or clearing account basis with countries also suffering shortages of foreign exchange, which discouraged efficiency and quality improvement. This situation was to change in the 1960s.

The 1960s and 1970s: Liberalization and Structural Change

In 1962 major economic reforms were announced. Once again the currency was devalued, this time from 1.80 Israeli pounds to the U.S. dollar to 3.00. The net devaluation was, however, much less than the 67 percent indicated by the formal change because almost all export subsidies were abolished and the rates of many tariffs on imports were lowered. The devaluation was also intended to unify the effective exchange rate system. This step was combined with a second major component of the new policy: liberalization of imports of consumer goods and some investment goods that had been excluded by quantitative restrictions (QRs). Most of this liberalization took the form of replacing QRs by tariffs (at different rates for each good) that were intended to be prohibitive, although some increase of liberalized imports did take place.[2]

During the 1960s the government's defense procurement program became an increasingly important means for encouraging industrial development. Elbit, Ltd., a computer company, was set up in 1966 as a partnership between the Ministry of Defense and Elron, Ltd. In the late 1950s and early 1960s the government became much more active in buying the shares of companies that were going bankrupt. In 1966 the Ministry of Industry and Trade asked Israel Military Industries to buy Ilin, a defense manufacturer. After attempts to sell the company to other private investors had failed, the Ministry of Defense purchased it.

Between the 1967 and 1973 wars, industry received a major boost as a result of defense developments. A French embargo on arms supplies to Israel led the government to encourage domestic production of weapons systems on a much larger scale than before. France had, until 1967, been Israel's major arms supplier; the gap caused by the embargo was a large one.

Research, development, and production of a wide range of high-technology defense products started after the 1967 war. There were also spin-offs in civilian production. Industrial production grew rapidly, particularly in the metals, electronics, and electrical appliances industries. The Israel Defense Forces (IDF) was able both to impose high standards and to test products.

In the late 1960s industrial policy was reinforced by the creation of the Office of Chief Scientist in a number of ministries. Most important was that in the Ministry of Industry and Trade, which from 1968/69 on received a budget for investment in industrial research and development projects that could lead to exports. The emphasis on defense industries and research and development in electronics and other industries led to a rapid growth of exports. Total exports increased threefold between 1966 and 1973 in current prices. Those of the more sophisticated high-technology sector, which had relatively high levels of research and development, increased tenfold.

Since the late 1960s the chief scientist at the Ministry of Industry and Trade has provided funding for industrial research and development programs and has assisted in the development of knowledge-based industries. These are industries for which the use of educated manpower is often more important than inputs of fixed capital. The Investment Center, in the same ministry, under the Law for the Encouragement of Capital Investment, continues to subsidize fixed capital investment. In so doing it still reflects the economic philosophy of the 1950s and 1960s.

Despite moves toward liberalization in foreign trade, the government played an increasing role in the ownership of companies. For instance, in 1965 the government bought shares in Polgat, a major clothing manufacturer. This policy of increased government activity in support of industry resulted in a larger number of companies being wholly or partially owned by the state. In 1961 there were seventy-five such firms; in 1968 there were 137.

The 1980s

The government signed trade agreements with the European Community (EC) and the United States in 1975 and 1985, respectively. These agreements have been the most significant features of a long-term liberalization of the economy, a move from import substitution toward reliance on exports as the motor of growth (see Chapter 5).

The emphasis on exports was reinforced by the government's provision, since 1981, of compensation for the lag between changes in the exchange rate and that of consumer prices. In 1989 this compensation was worth between $400 million and $500 million.

In July 1985 the emphasis of economic policy shifted toward reducing inflation by freezing the exchange rate, first against the dollar and later against a basket of currencies. This change resulted in a real increase in the value of the shekel against the dollar, which particularly penalized exports of the high-technology sector. The policy of a frozen exchange rate implied that firms should control their own wage costs and not expect a devaluation to compensate for local cost increases. The government reduced the value of industrial subsidies and has gradually been trying to open the capital market to the private sector. Reductions in income tax have been designed to increase incentives.

Industrial Structure

The Pattern of Ownership

There are three main types of industrial ownership in Israel: the government-owned sector, most of which has been developed since 1948; that belonging to the Histadrut (the General Federation of Labor), with its origins in the 1920s; and the private sector. The government and Histadrut each account for about 25 percent of industry in terms of income, and the private sector for 50 percent. The private sector owned more than 95 percent of factories and plants throughout the period 1965–1981 because virtually all small businesses were privately owned. Changes in the pattern of ownership between the periods 1965–1967 and 1980–1981 are illustrated in Table 4.1 and are examined in the sections below.

The Public Sector

There are three main kinds of government enterprises. The first is the group of companies and authorities that operate as integral parts of the

TABLE 4.1
Changes in Industrial Ownership, 1965-1981
(percent)

	1965-1967	1971-1972	1980-1981
By output			
Private sector	72	66	54
Histadrut	16	19	22
Public sector	12	15	24
Total	100	100	100
By employment			
Private sector	76	73	66
Histadrut	14	15	18
Public sector	10	12	16
Total	100	100	100

Source: A. Bregman, Industry and Industrial Policy, 1965-1985, Jerusalem: Bank of Israel, Research Department, 1986.

government apparatus. These include the lands authority and some parts of the military industries. Others are statutory authorities: the Bank of Israel, the ports and airports authorities, as well as some agricultural marketing authorities. Finally, there are corporations, including many industrial ones, over which the government has control. In 1989 there were 159 such enterprises, ninety-three of them government enterprises (with thirty-six subsidiaries), and thirty joint ventures of the government and the private sector or Histadrut, in which the state had a minority share holding. They employed 62,000 people in 1989 and had a total income of about $8 billion. Net profits came to $200 million, a rate of return on capital of 4.7 percent. Exports equalled $2.7 billion.[3]

Government-owned companies are mainly responsible for raw material exploitation, under the framework of Israel Chemical Industries, and development of the economic infrastructure for industry, agriculture, and tourism. Public utilities are responsible for water, electricity, telecommunications, and air and maritime transportation. Israel Aircraft Industries, the country's largest industrial company, is also government owned. Government companies are involved in oil exploration, construction, housing, and tourist development. These firms are formally obliged to operate according to business criteria unless the government, with the approval of the Knesset's Finance Committee, decides otherwise. Their share in total industrial output doubled between the periods 1965–1967 and 1980–1981, and their share in employment rose by 60 percent, largely due to the expansion of Israel Aircraft Industries.

The Cooperative Sector

The Histadrut, through its holding company Hevrat Ovdim (The Workers' Company), owns a wide range of enterprises in most sectors of the economy. Its 1985 turnover was $3.7 billion, a quarter of total industrial sales. Exports came to $895 million, investments were $365 million, and it employed 56,000 people.[4] Its main industrial holding is Koor, the largest holding company in the country, with sales in 1989 of about $2.3 billion and with 33,000 workers employed in 100 factories.[5] Koor owns some of the largest companies in the electronics sector, including Tadiran and Telrad, respectively Israel's second largest industrial company and its largest telecommunications company. The concern owns large parts of the metals sector and is involved in the food, consumer goods, chemicals, plastics, rubber, and minerals industries.

The relationship between the individual companies and Hevrat Ovdim varies. Tadiran, for example, is run independently, while other companies in the electronics and electrical division are much less free of control by Koor, Hevrat Ovdim, and ultimately the Histadrut. Koor has a number of joint ventures with kibbutzim and also with the private sector and foreign investors. The financial and ideological problems now being faced by many companies belonging to the Histadrut are examined in Chapter 7. The share of total industrial output produced by Histadrut companies increased by 6 percent and their share in industrial employment rose by 4 percent between the periods 1965–1967 and 1980–1981.

The Private Sector

Much of the private sector is owned by a number of holding companies, some of which are themselves interlinked. The Clal Group, which was founded by a group of Latin American businessmen in the 1960s at the initiative of the government, is one of the largest. Through Clal Industries, it has shareholdings in a wide range of companies in the electronics, metals, food, clothing, textiles, and cement industries. It also controls a financing company and has leasing, insurance, property development, and data processing subsidiaries. The Clal Group's 1985 sales were $822 million, and it had 13,000 employees.[6] Although it is considered to be a private sector conglomerate, 41 percent of Clal's shares are owned by Bank Hapoalim, which is part of the Histadrut. Discount Investment Corporation, Ltd., owned by Israel's largest private banking group, controls 34 percent of the shares in Clal and has shareholdings in a wide range of other companies. Income from companies in which Discount owned more than 5 percent of the shares exceeded $1.2 billion in December 1985, and its exports totalled $414 million. Clal and Discount together had sales of $2 billion, equal to about 8 percent of gross national product (GNP).

Between the periods 1965–1967 and 1980–1981 the private sector's share in total industrial output fell by 18 percent, and its share in industrial employment fell by 10 percent. These changes reflected the strength of the government and Histadrut sectors, despite the moves toward a more market-orientated economy.

The rest of the private sector is dominated by a number of long-established, family-owned companies, many of which have monopolies in the local market. The development of Elite, Ltd., provides an interesting example of the way in which part of the private sector developed. The company was founded in 1934 by eight businessmen from Latvia. Elite did particularly well during the Second World War, supplying the Allied Forces in the Middle East. After the foundation of the state, rationing was introduced and the company was permitted to use its export revenues to fund production for the local market. The import of new machinery from West Germany was made possible by reparations payments, and expertise for chocolate production was purchased from Switzerland. With the government's permission, Elite bought a number of smaller local chocolate producers. In 1973 the company went public, with members of the founding families maintaining control of a company that had originally been founded with an investment of 50,000 pounds.

After years of monopoly in the chocolate market, Elite now faces competition from a subsidiary of Koor. It has diversified into other areas of production, the most important of which is coffee, in which it has a near monopoly (see "Monopoly and Competition" below). In 1988 its turnover was $195 million.

Elite is also an example of how business-government relations operated in Israel. In each sphere of its activities the firm was involved in negotiations with the government. Foreign currency for imported machinery came from the reparations negotiated by the government. In the 1950s, when chocolate was considered by the government to be a luxury good, Elite was given permission to supply the local market on the condition that it attempted to export as well.

The Main Sectors of Industry

There have been considerable changes in the structure of industry over the last twenty years (see Table 4.2). The shares of textiles, clothing, and

TABLE 4.2
Sectoral Composition of Industrial Output and Exports, 1970 and 1990
(percent)

	Output		Exports	
	1970	1990 [a]	1970	1990 [a]
Food, tobacco and drinks	21.4	20.2	9.0	6.2
Textiles, clothing and leather	15.1	7.4	11.3	7.4
Wood, paper and printing	10.3	11.2	5.5	8.0
Quarrying and mining	6.8	5.7	5.2	2.8
Chemicals, rubber and plastic	10.9	16.1	17.4	17.0
Metals and machinery	16.8	13.9	6.2	10.7
Electricals and electronics	6.4	12.6	1.7	15.1
Transport equipment	5.7	4.0	1.4	5.6
Diamonds	6.6	8.9	42.3	27.2
Total	100.0	100.0	100.0	100.0

[a] Estimates

Sources: 1980:Industry in Israel 1988, Jerusalem: Ministry of Industry and Trade, Center for Planning and Economics, 1989.1990: Ministry of Industry Budget 1991, Jerusalem: Ministry of Finance, December 1990.

leather nearly halved; chemicals, rubber, and plastics rose by nearly 40 percent; and electronics and electrical equipment doubled. Transport equipment declined in importance but that of diamonds rose. In exports the most dramatic increase was in electronics and electrical equipment. Traditional industries such as diamonds, food, textiles, clothing, and leather all declined. Export performance, therefore, reflected that of output but on an exaggerated scale.

The Chemical Industry

The chemical industry is based on the mineral resources of the Dead Sea and the Negev, Israel's southern desert. The Dead Sea Works dates back to the 1920s; Israel Chemical Industries was set up as a state holding company in 1967. It is a very profitable group of companies involved in extracting, refining, and exporting nonmetallic minerals, derivatives, and products. It produces a wide range of chemicals and fertilizers. The Dead Sea Works extracts potash, and one of its main subsidiaries extracts and refines bromide. Israel's success in the international potash market is a function of its abundant and high-quality raw materials, modern technology, successful management, and marketing strategy.

The organic chemical industry has been less successful, partly because of the lack of local natural resources. Until recently it was completely controlled by the government on a cost-plus basis, which prevented the development of economies of scale and thus of lower costs, thereby severely constraining international competitiveness. The industry is also much less integrated than its competitors abroad: There are a relatively large number of small companies. With government encouragement a new ethylene and polyethylene company was set up in the late 1980s, which will in part rationalize the industry.

The chemical industry is the largest net exporter in Israel; its 1990 sales were estimated at $1.8 billion. Value added, at nearly 100 percent in most subsectors, is much higher than the average in Israeli industry and so the net contribution of exports is much greater than that of other sectors. Israel Chemical Industries had sales of $1.2 billion in 1990, and exports equalled $646 million.[7]

In the related field of rubber and plastics, exports were estimated at $324 million in 1989.[8] The pharmaceutical industry is dominated by one company, Teva, which in 1988 had sales of $211 million and exports of $82 million.

The Food Industry

With an estimated 1990 output of about $5.4 billion, the food industry is the largest in the country. It employs 50,000 people but had a low rate of value added of about 20 percent. Exports were $570 million in 1989.[9]

The industry has benefited from developments in agriculture, particularly as a result of the diversification of production. Its exports are limited by the relatively high cost of water and labor. The industry has succeeded in supplying a large share of local needs: In 1980 imports accounted for only 10 percent of local demand, although this rate was partly due to government restrictions on what could be brought into the country.

In the absence of abundant water and cheap labor, the food industry has been dependent on the development of new products and on close cooperation with agriculture. Raw materials are both locally produced and imported; about 60 percent of gross output and 80 percent of exports are based on local agricultural output.

Textiles and Clothing

The textile and clothing industries were set up in the 1950s and 1960s to meet the basic needs of the population and to provide employment in development towns. With government support and behind protective barriers, a number of firms began to dominate the local market. As the economy was opened up to foreign trade, exports became increasingly necessary, but because of the orientation of much of the industry, its products were not suited for sale abroad. In order to export products, quality control and marketing had to be improved. These steps were not easy or even possible for a number of the older companies, but two firms, Polgat and Delta, became large clothing exporters. Part of their comparative advantage lay in low labor costs, increasingly sophisticated design, improved technology, and successful marketing. Polgat and Delta developed close links with foreign purchasers, most notably with Marks and Spencer in the United Kingdom, which advised them on quality control.

In 1990 this sector employed 44,000 workers and its total output came to $1.8 billion. A slump in both domestic and foreign demand has resulted in exports stagnating for three years and a 19 percent fall in the number of employees in the industry. In 1990 exports recovered to $780 million.

Diamonds

The diamond industry was founded in 1939 when, as a result of the outbreak of World War II, contact was broken between Belgium and South Africa, then the centers of the industry. A group of Belgian and local entrepreneurs came together to start the industry in Netanya, north of Tel Aviv. Net exports increased from $12 million in 1950 to $2.9 billion in 1990, but value added, at about 15 percent, is very low: Most of the value of a polished diamond exported from Israel is accounted for by the imported, rough stone. The local addition is in the value of the cutting. Special income tax arrangements apply to the industry, making it in effect an off-shore sector, but it is not clear if the subsidy for the employment of 11,000 workers, through tax concessions, is beneficial to the economy as a whole.

Electronics and High Technology

There is a considerable overlap between the electronics and high-technology sectors and the military industries analyzed in Chapter 2. The focus here is on the characteristics of civilian production. In 1990 the electronics and electrical sector had 90,000 employees.

The most significant trend in Israeli industry in recent years has been the development of products through local research and their sale abroad. This trend is especially true of electronics. Exports of electronic and electrical goods came to $1.6 billion in 1990. In 1968 exports of goods based on local research and development came to less than $200 million;

by 1985 they had reached $2 billion, in current prices. Their share in total industrial exports (excluding diamonds) rose from 22 percent to about 40 percent during this period. This sector made a major contribution to the internationalization of the economy. It brought rapid developments in production technology and marketing and made use of highly skilled workers. It also accounted for a large share of expenditures on research and development. It is not easy to categorize firms in the industry, but electronics includes medical, communications, and military equipment, as well as computerized systems for irrigation and energy. Companies involved in these activities have been characterized until recently by fast growth. For example, Scitex, a manufacturer of color imaging machinery, whose products are among the most sophisticated of their type in the world, increased its sales from $4.3 million in 1975 to $352 million in 1990. Another example is Elscint, a producer of medical machinery, which increased its exports from $1 million in 1969/70 to $147 million in 1985. Tadiran's growth and development also fit this pattern.

Many of these companies were founded by engineers with a production rather than marketing orientation. They played a very important role in an economic environment that makes entrepreneurial activity difficult. In the civilian field, the generation of new ideas and products led to successful sales in niche markets overseas that larger foreign companies would not find worthwhile supplying. Flexibility in design and production are among Israel's competitive advantages; most significant for many small firms is their willingness and ability to produce small batches.[10] The marketing effort to back this capacity has been weak, however. Success has depended on growth in the market and the supply of new products, which in turn requires expensive outlays on research and development. When the international electronics market went into recession in the mid-1980s, mainly because of oversupply, most of these companies ran into difficulties. The industry, like others in Israel, suffers from being isolated from its markets abroad, the most important of which is the United States. Production-oriented management has had difficulties in adapting to market changes; a lack of marketing skills is a major problem in Israel. The lack of a large domestic market limits the ability of industry to mass produce and attain economies of scale. By 1990 Scitex, Elscint, and Tadiran had undergone major reorganizations under new management, and their sales were increasing again.

The electronics industry, which constitutes the main part of the high-technology sector, has experienced rapid growth. A further benefit for the economy is that total value added in electronics is between 50 percent and 60 percent, higher than the all-industry average. Exports also account for the larger-than-average share of its output.

Factors Influencing Industrial Performance

Research, Development, and Skilled Manpower

The existence of the electronics and high-technology sectors was made possible by investment in research and development (R&D) and by a growing supply of skilled labor. Israel has one of the highest ratios of gross domestic expenditure on R&D to GNP in the world. In 1983 it was 3.04 percent compared to 2.7 percent in the United States and 2.6 percent in Japan. The absolute volume of R&D was small (at $707 million in 1983) compared to West Germany, for example ($18.1 billion), and much of it was devoted to military projects, some of which resulted in exports.

In 1968 the economic benefits were acknowledged with the establishment of a budget for investment in R&D in the chief scientist's office at the Ministry of Industry and Trade. Its annual budget is about $100 million. Other ministries have their own chief scientists' offices with much smaller budgets. The Ministry of Science and Development, through the National Council for Research and Development, has a small budget for basic research.[11] Total government spending on R&D in the 1986/87 budget was $220 million.

The government has played a major role in technological development. It set up the Israel Standards Institute, promoted "buy national" campaigns, permitted accelerated depreciation, encouraged foreign investment, set up industrial research institutes and the Productivity Institute, and assisted in export marketing programs, partly through the Export Institute. It also assists in obtaining patents, negotiates international trade agreements, invests in education and training, and has encouraged the development of management education.

The universities have played a major part in increasing the supply of qualified engineers and technicians in industry from 11,500 in 1972 to 30,800 in 1984. The number of engineers per thousand employees in industry increased from eight in 1965 to about thirty-three in 1982. The increase in overall skilled manpower was even more dramatic in the high-technology sector, where human capital was the sine qua non.

As a result of the investment in education, especially at the higher level, and the allocation of funds for research, Israel has a high ratio of graduates to nongraduates in the labor force. In 1983, 13 percent of the labor force had academic degrees compared to 7.6 percent in 1973. The number of professionals working in research and development in 1969/70 was 886; in 1984/85 it was 3,260.[12] There has also been an increase in the share and absolute number of workers who are classified as scientific, academic, professional, and technical from 284,000 in 1980 (22.6 percent of all employed workers) to 359,000 (24.6 percent) in 1989.[13]

In 1985/86 $835 million was spent on civilian R&D; 35 percent of this amount was funded by the government, and 50 percent of R&D was carried out in industry and agriculture. There has also been foreign assistance in the finance of R&D. In 1977 the Israeli and United States governments set up the Bilateral Industrial Research and Development Foundation (BIRD-F). By 1988 it had $110 million in endowment funds that were contributed jointly by the two governments, and by the end of the U.S. fiscal year 1988 it had provided funds for 182 joint American-Israeli projects, which had resulted in sales totalling $150 million.[14] Binational science and industry agreements, modelled on BIRD-F, have been signed with a number of European countries.

In the mid-1980s there was a slump in much of the high-technology sector as a result of an international recession in the industry and a reduction in local defense orders. Although there is a consensus that these are the industries of the future, technological development and managerial improvements are leading to growth in traditional sectors such as clothing and textiles. By 1990 there was a recovery in the high-technology sector: Firms were adapting to the harsher economic environment by laying off workers and by increasing their marketing efforts abroad.

Foreign Investment

Despite its very small volume, foreign investment has been qualitatively very important. In 1988 it totalled $289 million, or about 2 percent of total investment. Much of it took the form of purchases of shares in Israeli companies.

In the electronics sector a number of foreign companies, nearly all of them American, set up sales offices or agencies in Israel. One of the largest of this type of investment was carried out by Motorola. Others, such as National Semi-Conductors and Intel, set up research and development centers, and another group founded research, development, and production facilities together. The most common pattern, however, was to start with sales offices, or research and development projects, and then move into production. The most successful foreign investments have been based on the use of Israeli research and development in high technology. This type of investment has succeeded largely because of the availability of very highly skilled labor.

Much of this investment has been based on a Jewish connection that helped to mitigate the effects of the Arab boycott, or at least the boycott's strength as perceived in the West. Partnerships between Israeli and foreign companies have not been prominent or usually successful, nor has the day-to-day management of Israeli companies by foreigners. In a number of cases the foreign investor has come to live permanently in Israel and manage the investment himself; the most important example of this was Polgat. Foreign involvement in such companies as Tadiran, the Ashdod bus plant, Bet Shemesh Aircraft Engines, and Elbit provided technology, marketing, and other management skills, even though the foreign connections were eventually reduced or ended.

The government continues to offer grants and tax concessions to foreign investors. The extent of these benefits depends on the location of the potential plant and its export prospects. The foreign investment program that was originally designed in the 1950s to generate employment in the development towns has shifted toward exports. Foreign investors have been constrained by the Arab boycott, war and tension in the Middle East, inflation, high taxation, and a high level of government interference and economic uncertainty in Israel. Those firms that have invested have, however, achieved considerable success, and their Israeli subsidiaries have become important parts of the companies as a whole. In 1985 there were 100 U.S. companies with subsidiaries in Israel, one-quarter of which were in high-technology research and development and/or production.

Monopoly and Competition

Monopolies and other restrictive practices are very important features of Israel's economy. They have been important sources of continued inflation and have contributed to the problems of slow growth. In 1989 35 percent of goods and services were supplied by monopolies.[15] In addition to those sectors and industries that are monopolized in many other countries, there are others that lack competition for specifically Israeli reasons. There has never been an overall consensus or policy with regard to monopoly, oligopoly, or other restrictive practices.

According to an official survey, in 1984 sales of the three largest firms in each industrial branch accounted for 49 percent of total sales, compared with, for example, 24 percent in France, 20 percent in Italy, and 34 percent in Belgium. On a subbranch basis, sales of the largest four firms accounted for 60 percent of sales in Israel, compared to 50 percent in the United States and the EC. An important reason for this concentration was and is the relationship between the optimal size of the plant and the size of the local market.[16] The small size of Israeli markets often makes it feasible to have only one producer.

Another important set of influences has been the behavior of firms and the government. Tariffs, other restrictions, taxes on imports, as well as high transport costs for imports to Israel result in high costs for many commodities in the economy. If imports were liberalized, then economies of scale and other competitive advantages that exist abroad would have a much greater impact on the Israeli economy. As a result, much production in Israel would be less profitable than it now is, under protected conditions. The minimum plant size needed to achieve the economies of scale realized abroad would rise to levels that local markets could not support. For this reason, among others, local production of many items might cease. New industries, based on local competitive advantages, would be needed to replace those that closed. It is this process of competitive change, with its uncertainties and risks, that many are naturally afraid of. Much of what the government does is therefore designed to maintain the status quo.

The granting of monopolies was a method by which the government encouraged private investment. In return for granting a private company the monopoly, the government was promised investment, employment, and exports. Returning to the example of Elite, this company now has 50 percent of the local non–instant coffee market. The owners of its main domestic competitor also have a substantial shareholding in Elite. Two main European suppliers control 80 percent of the instant coffee market; one of them owns 40 percent of the shares in a company associated with Elite. Imports of the other main European brands are handled by a company whose owner holds 11 percent of Elite's shares. As a result of these factors, the whole market for coffee is highly uncompetitive, even before the question of import duties is considered.[17] This situation is not atypical of Israeli markets.

The degree of monopoly has been particularly high in those sectors for which large-scale capital investment was required; having competing producers in a small home market has often been considered uneconomical. One of the most recent examples has been the Mazlat, a pilotless airplane, or drone (see Chapter 3). A counterexample was the decision of the government, after intense debate, to have two suppliers of digital telephone exchanges.

The restriction of imports has been an important way of maintaining a privileged position for local producers. In addition, importers are licensed, and frequently only one is permitted for each product. The result is that even where the volume of imports is below that demanded by the market (which, other things being equal, pushes up prices), the importer gets the further benefit of a monopoly price. The high prices that result on domestic markets have led to the widespread, and semitolerated, smuggling of basic goods, such as clothing, by thousands of Israelis returning from trips abroad. The losses in customs duties are worth millions of dollars.[18]

The continued protection of many industries enables them to obtain monopoly profits. The rate of increase of prices of goods and services supplied by monopolies was higher than that of the consumer price index in 1989. This protectionism has been an important factor contributing to high inflation during a period of recession.[19]

Table 4.3
Indicators of Growth in Industry, 1968-1989
(real average annual change, percent, excluding diamonds)

	1968-72	1973-79	1980-85	1986-89
Industrial production	15.1	4.9	2.6	0.8
Labor input [a]	9.1	0.6	0.5	-2.2
Capital input [b]	6.5	7.6	4.8	3.2
Production per man-day	5.5	4.3	2.1	3.0
Total factor productivity [c]	7.0	1.4	0.6	1.1
Industrial exports [d]	16.6	11.1	9.3	6.7

[a] Man-days
[b] Beginning-of-year stock
[c] Product per weighted unit of capital and labor. The weight of labor is 58 percent.
[d] Excluding exports to administered territories

Sources: 1968-1979: A. Bregman, Industry and Industrial Policy in Israel, 1965-1985, Jerusalem: Bank of Israel, Research Department 1986.
1980-1985: Annual Report, 1988, Jerusalem: Bank of Israel,1989.
1986-1989: Annual Report, 1989, Jerusalem: Bank of Israel,1990.

The Slowdown in Growth

Table 4.3 shows the growth of industrial output between 1968 and 1989. Since the period 1968–1972, it has decelerated substantially; in 1988, for only the second time in the last thirty years, there was actually a fall in output; something that continued in 1989. This slowdown has been the central problem in the Israeli economy since 1973.

Industry has been considered the leading sector of the economy, largely because of its export capacity. Exports increased their share of output but did not grow at a rapid enough rate to consistently push up total output. The dramatic rise in the share of exports in industrial output between 1965 and 1989 is shown in Table 4.4.

Long-run factors combined with short-term ones to cause the slowdown. The rate of population growth slowed down in the 1960s and 1970s, thus reducing the rate of growth of demand for industry's products and labor supply. The growth of the labor force in industry was further constrained by the growth of employment in the public sector. In 1970, 219,000 people were employed in public and community services, which

TABLE 4.4
Destination of Industrial Output, 1965-1989
(percent)

	1965	1975	1985	1989
Private consumption	46	25	23	26
Public consumption	7	19	15	14
Investment	27	19	13	13
Exports	20	37	49	47
Total	100	100	100	100

Sources: 1965 and 1975: A. Bregman, Industry and Industrial Policy in Israel, 1965-1985, Jerusalem: Bank of Israel, Research Department, 1986.
1985: Annual Report 1988, Jerusalem: Bank of Israel,1989.
1989: Annual Report 1989, Jerusalem: Bank of Israel,1990.

was nearly 22 percent of the labor force. By 1989 the number had risen to 429,000, or 29 percent.

As a result of the rise in oil and raw material prices in the years 1973/1974 and 1979/1980, less income was available for the purchase of locally made goods. In the periods 1975–1977 and 1979–1980 the government adopted contractionary economic policies, and from 1978 to 1985 hyperinflation made planning and investment problematic, if not impossible, for many companies. This situation was reflected in very volatile investment levels: Gross fixed investment in real terms rose by 10.3 percent in 1983 but fell in 1984 by 7.6 percent and in 1985 by 13.4 percent.

Until the early 1970s economic growth was sufficient to increase living standards without recourse to short-term international borrowing. Between 1973 and 1985 Israel's average annual rate of growth was less than 2 percent and per capita growth was close to zero. It is generally agreed that, at least until 1983, the major causes of the poor performance of the economy were the combined effects of the sharp increases in oil prices and defense spending.

The increase in public sector employment and rising welfare payments were financed by higher taxation, national insurance contributions, and deficit finance. The latter pushed up interest rates and thus industrial costs. Taxation and transfers from the public increased from 33.1 percent in 1970 to 49.3 percent in 1985. Although much of this amount was returned to the public in the form of transfers, the gross level of taxation affected incentives.

It has been estimated that half of the slowdown in output growth of the business sector between the period 1961–1972 and the period 1973–1981 was due to the slowdown in productivity growth and half was due to a slowdown in inputs of capital and labor.[20] The slowdown in productivity was in turn due to an imbalance between capital and labor growth: Inputs of capital grew even faster than output. This imbalance was due to the energy crisis, which made some of the capital stock outdated and forced its replacement, and subsidies on capital that encouraged excessive investment. In 1984 Israel spent the equivalent of 21.0 percent of GNP on investment in fixed assets, a greater share than the United States, the United Kingdom, Italy, France, Canada, or Sweden. Of the eight major non-Communist industrial countries, only Japan and West Germany had shares that exceeded that of Israel. The average capital stock per person employed rose in real terms by 24.6 percent between 1974 and 1984, that in the manufacturing industry by 79.4 percent. GDP per capita rose by only 3.7 percent, and real product per person employed increased by 26.3 percent, implying that additions to capital were not being efficiently used.[21] Excess capital stock and high income taxes meant that capital utilization fell: Workers had little incentive to do more than one shift, as the marginal rate of income tax that they paid on overtime rates for the second shift was high.[22]

From 1973 productivity growth in manufacturing declined more steeply than supplies of labor and capital. An estimated 78.5 percent of the decline in the growth of gross product in manufacturing industries between 1973 and 1983 was due to the fall in productivity growth rates.[23] Seventy-three percent of the difference in manufacturing industry productivity growth between the period 1965–1972 and the period 1972–1979 was accounted for by the decline in capital utilization.[24] This decline has been explained by excessive subsidies on capital, uncertainty generated by inflation, and adjustments to rising raw material prices, something that occurred in the United States, Japan, West Germany, the United Kingdom, and other countries. The capital stock in any period never fully matches current production plans; the former is a function of past decisions.

The deceleration in productivity growth, especially when measured by GDP per employed person, was greater in Israel than abroad because, until 1988, unemployment increased more slowly. Workers who probably would have been unemployed in North America or Western Europe were, in Israel, absorbed by the public sector. Industry shed fewer workers than abroad partly because of the strength of the Histadrut; publicly owned companies were subject to government control and the state has, until recently, been very strongly opposed to redundancies. While average unemployment in the Organization for Economic Cooperation and Development (OECD) region in 1981–1983 was 8.3 percent of the labor force, the comparable figure in Israel was 4.9 percent.[25] Output per employee in the economy is much lower in Israel than in many developed countries and its growth in recent years has been slower. Despite the low level of productivity growth, until 1989 real wages rose relatively rapidly, threatening the competitiveness of Israeli exports and permitting private consumption to grow faster than GNP.

An important question is why real wages rose more than productivity. Achieving peace with labor in conditions of full employment is one factor; another is that firms expected the government to compensate them for increased domestic costs by devaluation. It has been part of the industrial culture that firms have relied on the government to bail them out of problems, even those of their own creation. In June 1986 the director-general of the Ministry of Finance blamed competition between Israeli firms for the rising level of wages in the electronics industry.[26] Israeli high-technology companies face international competition for their more skilled labor: Israeli engineers and scientists are sometimes willing to move to the United States in search of higher remuneration. As a result some employees in Israel are paid a U.S. level of gross salary without the overall level of productivity to support it. The chairman of the Association of Electronic Industries, however, stated that wages rose because of government-Histadrut agreements that firms were obliged by law to implement, rather than because firms were competing for labor in a partly international market.[27]

Although wage costs are lower in many sectors than they are in electronics, very high levels of income tax contribute to a wide gap between gross and net pay, which means that labor is not cheap in most sectors. Employers also have many charges and benefits to pay beyond the basic salary. A comparison between the cost of an engineer (gross wage plus social and other benefits) and his gross and net pay in the United States and Israel is illustrative. For every dollar that the Israeli engineer received in net salary in 1985, his employer had to pay $2.88; in the United States the respective amount was $1.62. If pension, holidays, study leave, and other minor benefits are added to the net salary, then the relationship to gross rose to 79 percent in Israel and 84.5 percent in the United States. These additions are not, however, felt by the employee as earnings in the same way that net salary is. It is net pay that motivates employees; net pay constituted about one-third of the employers' total labor costs in Israel and two-thirds in the United States.[28]

The cost of hired labor is equal to two-thirds of gross product at factor cost; as a result changes in labor costs have profound effects on profitability. Between 1965–1967 and 1986–1988 the rate of return on capital fell from 12 percent to 6 percent. This decrease was largely the result of higher wage costs, which caused a 20 percent increase in the share of labor in industrial product.[29] Higher wage costs also caused a fall in investment in recent years that has been a cause of slower industrial and economic growth.[30]

The problems of productivity and competitiveness are also sectoral. If labor costs in the economy are high and productivity is low, then the level of exports should be low. This reasoning suggests that some sectors or firms have high productivity and relatively low cost advantages while others do not. The growing internationalization of the economy suggests that there are sectors that are internationally competitive and others that are much less so.

The cost structure of exports depends not only on the productivity of factors of production within the firm, but also on the incentives it receives. These include exchange rate insurance as well as credit subsidies and tax advantages made available to approved or authorized exporters. (The latter constituted 40 percent of all industrial firms in 1975.[31]) Each industry, firm, or product, therefore, could have an effective exchange rate of its own that is likely to be significantly different from the official one.

The deceleration of export growth can only partly be accounted for by the deceleration in international trade. It was much less than the slowdown in total output growth because of a change in the composition of output. In 1965 science-based industries, such as electronics, chemicals, transport equipment, metals, and machinery, accounted for 37 percent. By 1985 they took 56 percent. Their export growth rate between 1965 and 1984 was 16 percent in real terms, compared to 9 percent in traditional industries (food, textiles, clothing, wood, paper, printing, rubber, and plastics).

A problem in macroeconomic management has been the inability to achieve a real devaluation of the exchange rate for more than a short period. Indexation has meant that cost increases caused by a devaluation have always been passed on through the economy, with compensation eventually being paid to workers, owners of government stock, and others. The economy has, therefore, been trapped between inflation and balance-of-payments problems. The economic experience of many countries shows that devaluation has to be accompanied by a reduction in local demand in order to make room for increased exports. Improvements in corporate strategy, marketing, and management would make the pick up in exports quicker and more effective under such conditions. The dramatic reduction in inflation in the second half of 1985 was, to a great extent, a result of a temporary reduction in real wages. By the beginning of 1986 this gain had virtually disappeared; real wages were increasing again. Inflation, although low by Israeli standards, once again reduced the competitiveness of exports due to the fixed exchange rate and lower inflation in overseas markets. The problems of external competitiveness have been compounded by the lack of domestic competition.

Business sector profits have been squeezed in recent years, and their slight improvement, at the expense of labor in 1989, was not enough to compensate for the downward trend (figures on the shares of capital and labor in the national income are given in Chapter 7). Many companies have been undertaking programs to increase efficiency, but such efforts have involved making workers redundant rather than increasing investment. Large sectors of the economy, such as Koor, the kibbutzim, and the moshavim, have been in financial difficulties and have frozen or cut their investments. The domestic political situation, including a government crisis for three months in the spring of 1990, added to uncertainties about government policy in general and the exchange rate in particular. Finally, domestic demand from private and public consumption has been weak.

In 1990 industry made a modest recovery. Output rose by 6 percent compared with a 2 percent fall in 1989. Excluding the diamonds industry, the growth rate was 7.5 percent in 1990 and 3 percent in 1989. Most sectors were involved but those manufacturing for the building sector saw the fastest growth. Output in the building sector itself rose by 10 percent, double its 1989 rate, a direct result of the increase in immigration from the Soviet Union.

Agriculture

Agriculture developed in a very different way from industry. It was the focus of ideological interest in the prestate period; the goal of recreating a Jewish working class and reclaiming the Land of Israel from the desert dominated and was manifested in the establishment of kibbutzim. Following the creation of the state and the need to absorb large numbers of immigrants, many of whom were not disposed to communal living in kibbutzim, other forms of settlement were developed. These included moshavim (collectives) of various kinds.

Agricultural development has been successful in at least one major respect: Israel is in overall balance in food production. Although it has to import wheat and meat, as well as other items, its agricultural exports are large enough to cover the cost. This is a considerable achievement, given the growth of population and the lack of natural resources, especially water. It has also taken place in the context of a declining agricultural labor force and increased urbanization.

The development of agriculture since independence was marked by three phases. In the first, which lasted until 1960, demand exceeded supply and the first priority was to feed the population. This was a period of rapid demographic growth and the development of agriculture was natural. From 1960 to 1970 there was an element of oversupply, and planning had the more sophisticated task of balancing demand and supply, which was done by forecasting, without reliance on market forces.

Since 1970 the market mechanism has been used to balance supply and demand. In recent years there has been an increase in rural diversification: The kibbutzim in particular have been industrializing. Moshavim are now having to adjust to the fact that many of them are too small to be economically viable. Government intervention remains substantial through planning, rural settlement programs, research and development, extension services, and marketing functions. The state is also the sole importer of beef, sugar, grain, feed, and oil. It subsidizes the prices of water and land and provides agricultural credit.

Agricultural production rose sixteenfold between 1948/49 and 1984/85. The cultivated area increased by 65 percent. Between 1954/55 and 1984/85 employment in agriculture fell by 12.5 percent to 89,400.[32] Agriculture has become more capital intensive (measured in terms of capital per labor-hour worked), and output per hour worked has increased. In the period 1984–1985 it was 2.4 times its 1970–1972 level. The large productivity increase was the result of better levels of professional knowledge, experience, training, and research and development. Particularly important were improvements in the application of fertilizers, irrigation, and machinery.

In 1960 agriculture accounted for 12 percent of the net national product, 27 percent of fixed capital, and 17 percent of employment. In 1984 it represented 4 percent of output, 9 percent of fixed capital, and 6 percent of employment. In 1982/83 nearly one-third of agricultural production was used for local consumption and 25 percent for industrial consumption; 27 percent was directly exported and 2 percent was used in agriculture. Thirteen percent was used for purchased and intermediate inputs. Until 1986 agriculture became an increasingly traded sector, and it contributed to the balance of payments through higher exports of fresh and processed products. By 1988 the share of exported agricultural output had fallen to 19.3 percent, for reasons that are analyzed below. Imports of agricultural commodities and foodstuffs are very strictly controlled by the government: The free trade agreement with the United States permits imports of these goods; that with the EC is much more restrictive. Israeli producers, therefore, benefit from a protected home market.

Total agricultural production in 1989 was worth $2.8 billion. Inputs cost $1.6 billion and value added after depreciation was $900 million. In that year, $310 million was paid to employed labor and the income of the self-employed totalled $650 million.[33] Fixed factors of production included 2.4 million dunams (one dunam equals 1000 square meters) of irrigated land, 1.64 million dunams of nonirrigated land, and 1,410 billion cubic meters of water use a year.

Israel has lost its competitive position in the production of citrus and cotton as cheaper sources of supply became available. Its competitive advantage lies in having milder winters than in northern and western Europe, which are its main market. It also has lower labor costs in the production of vegetables, flowers, and citrus (except in orchards belonging to the kibbutzim). In both of these respects, it faces increased competition from developing Mediterranean countries. It has been able to introduce new products very successfully on the basis of research and development, but this innovation is now threatened by budget cuts in the public sector.

In the last few years agriculture has been subject to a number of crises. First it has suffered from the increase in real interest rates that has occurred since 1985. Prior to that date numerous investments were made on the basis of loans taken at negative real interest rates. Local purchasing organizations belonging to the moshav movement (which accounted for 40 percent of agricultural output) invested in plants without a national plan and adequate financial control. So, to a lesser extent, did the kibbutzim. Duplication between regional organizations for purchasing and processing agricultural commodities led to overcapacity. The increase in interest rates caused many of these projects to collapse financially. A similar process also occurred among private investments made by individual farmers.

A second factor that reduced incomes was the fall in international prices of seed products such as rice, maize, and cotton. As a result of the green revolution in Southeast Asia, those countries reduced their imports, causing international prices to fall by up to one-third in the late 1980s and early 1990s.

Unfavorable local weather conditions caused hundreds of millions of dollars of damage in 1988. In the early winter there was an almost unprecedented frost and in May of that year there was an unusually severe heat wave.

Difficult adjustments are now being made that may result in further reductions in agricultural employment and the closure of some moshavim. Israel's main overseas market is becoming more competitive. There are quotas on agricultural exports to the EC that limit Israeli sales, and an improvement in political relations will be necessary before these are eased or lifted altogether.

Agriculture and the Water Problem

Agriculture uses nearly 70 percent of Israel's annual water supply. The government allocates water to agriculture at heavily subsidized prices, which has encouraged overuse. As a result the natural water aquifers are being damaged, and there is the threat that seawater is being absorbed in coastal regions. This situation will have very damaging effects on agricultural land if the process is not halted.

Israel relies on modest rainfall and the flow of water into rivers in the north of the country to cover its needs. Considerable investments were made in the 1960s in a national water carrier to take water from Lake Kinneret in the Galilee to the center of the country and to the southern Negev desert. In the past twenty years, despite increased demand, there has been a lack of investment, the effects of which are now being felt. Agriculture as the major consumer will have to take on most of the burden of adjustment: Drastic reductions in its water use will be needed in the near future if the country is not to suffer even more serious shortages. The Ministry of Agriculture is responsible for managing the nation's water resources and has not yet taken the advice given by hydrologists several years ago, in a major report, on the need for change.[34] As a result, a large question mark hangs over the future pattern of production in agriculture.

Conclusion

The business sector as a whole, and agriculture and industry in particular, benefitted from extensive government assistance in their development. They were gradually encouraged to become more self-reliant, but even today, after major cuts in 1985, they receive considerable assistance and protection. Although the social costs of economic adjustment will be considerable, reductions in subsidies and protection are preconditions for growth.

Notes

1. N. Halevi and R. Klinov-Malul, *The Economic Development of Israel* (New York: Praeger and Bank of Israel, 1968), p. 132.
2. M. Michaely, *Foreign Trade Regimes: Israel* (New York: National Bureau for Economic Research, 1975), pp. 58–80.
3. *Report and Accounts for the Year 1989* (Jerusalem: Ministry of Finance, Government Corporations Authority, 1990). In Hebrew.
4. *Economic Report 1985* (Tel Aviv: Hevrat Ovdim, 1986), p. 13. In Hebrew.
5. *Ha'aretz* (Tel Aviv), 21 June 1990. In Hebrew.
6. *Annual Report 1985* (Tel Aviv: Clal Industries, Ltd., 1985). In Hebrew.
7. *Ha'aretz*, 23 April 1991. In Hebrew.
8. *Budget Proposal: Ministry of Industry and Trade 1990* (Jerusalem: Ministry of Finance, 1990). In Hebrew.
9. *Budget Proposal: Ministry of Industry and Trade 1990.*
10. S. Hirsch, "Technological Factors in the Composition and Direction of Israel's Industrial Exports," in S. Hirsch, ed., *The Technological Factor in International Trade* (New York: NBER, 1970).

11. *Scientific Research in Israel 1986* (Jerusalem: Ministry of Science and Development, National Council for Research and Development, June 1986).

12. Ibid.

13. *Statistical Abstract of Israel 1990* (Jerusalem: Central Bureau of Statistics, 1990).

14. *Status Report 1988* (Tel Aviv: Bilateral Industrial Research and Development Foundation, 1988).

15. *Ha'aretz,* 12 September 1989. In Hebrew.

16. *Patterns of Competition in Israeli Industry* (Jerusalem: Ministry of Industry and Trade, Supervisor of Restrictive Practices, 1984). In Hebrew.

17. *Ha'aretz,* 12 April 1989. In Hebrew.

18. *Ha'aretz,* 15 September 1989. In Hebrew.

19. *Ha'aretz,* 12 September 1989. In Hebrew.

20. J. Metzer, *The Slowdown of Economic Growth in Israel: A Passing Phase or the End of the Big Spurt?* (Jerusalem: Falk Institute, 1986).

21. A. Bregman, *The Slowdown of Industrial Productivity: Causes, Explanations and Surprises* (Jerusalem: Bank of Israel, Research Department Review, April 1985).

22. Y. Kondor, "Capital Utilization, Economies of Scale and Productivity in the Business Sector 1964–1980," *Economic Quarterly,* vol. 28, no. 110–111 (Tel Aviv, November 1981). In Hebrew. The 1981 figure was estimated by Metzer in *The Slowdown of Economic Growth in Israel.*

23. Metzer, *The Slowdown of Economic Growth in Israel.*

24. Bregman, *The Slowdown of Industrial Productivity.*

25. *Economic Outlook* (Paris: Organization for Economic Cooperation and Development [OECD], Historical Series 1969–81, no. 34, December 1984).

26. E. Sharon at Conference of the Budget Department of the Ministry of Finance, Jerusalem, January 1987.

27. Y. Neeman at Conference of the Budget Department of the Ministry of Finance, Jerusalem, January 1987.

28. *Asakim,* supplement to *Ma'ariv* (Tel Aviv), 4 February 1986. In Hebrew.

29. *Annual Report 1988* (Jerusalem: Bank of Israel, 1989). In Hebrew.

30. M. Bruno, "Israel's Crisis and Economic Reform in Historical Perspective," *Economic Quarterly,* vol. 40, no. 141 (Tel Aviv, 1989).

31. Bregman, *The Slowdown of Industrial Productivity.*

32. S. Pohoryles, *Agriculture in Israel. A Model of Economic Planning* (Tel Aviv: Hakibbutz Hameuchad, 1972). In Hebrew.

33. *Annual Report 1988* (Jerusalem: Bank of Israel, 1989). In Hebrew.

34. *Ha'aretz,* 15 May 1990. In Hebrew.

5

The International Sector

Israel has faced problems in the balance of payments since 1948 because imports of goods and services have always exceeded exports. Figure 5.1 shows the main developments since 1970. Large deficits in the mid-1970s and in the period 1978–1984 resulted in serious crises. Since 1985 unilateral transfers, mainly consisting of U.S. aid, financed the deficit on goods and services, and as a result there have been small surpluses in the current account in a number of years (see Tables 5.1 and 5.2).

There are many factors behind the balance-of-payments problems. Table 5.3 shows how the bill for imported fuel increased at the same time as the defense burden did. These factors worsened both the capital account as well as the current account; they caused an increase in international borrowing and debt financing. The table also illustrates how the slowdown in the growth of world trade, after the oil price rises of the years 1973–1974 and 1979–1980, made it harder for Israel to increase exports.

Israel's International Trade

The Import Surplus

Imports and exports have both grown rapidly as shares of gross national product (GNP) during the past forty years, but deficits on the trade account increased dramatically. In 1949 Israeli exports of goods covered 11.3 percent of the import bill for goods. In 1990 the coverage was 78 percent, but in volume terms the gap—$2.3 billion—remained large.

During the 1960s and 1970s emphasis was increasingly placed on exports as a means of generating economic growth and independence. Export growth rates exceeded those of imports, but because of the larger base of the latter a deficit remained. From the mid-1970s an increasing share of the overall deficit was accounted for by military and oil imports and debt servicing. The years up to 1972 were, in the main, ones of fast

Figure 5.1 The Balance of Payments, 1970-1990

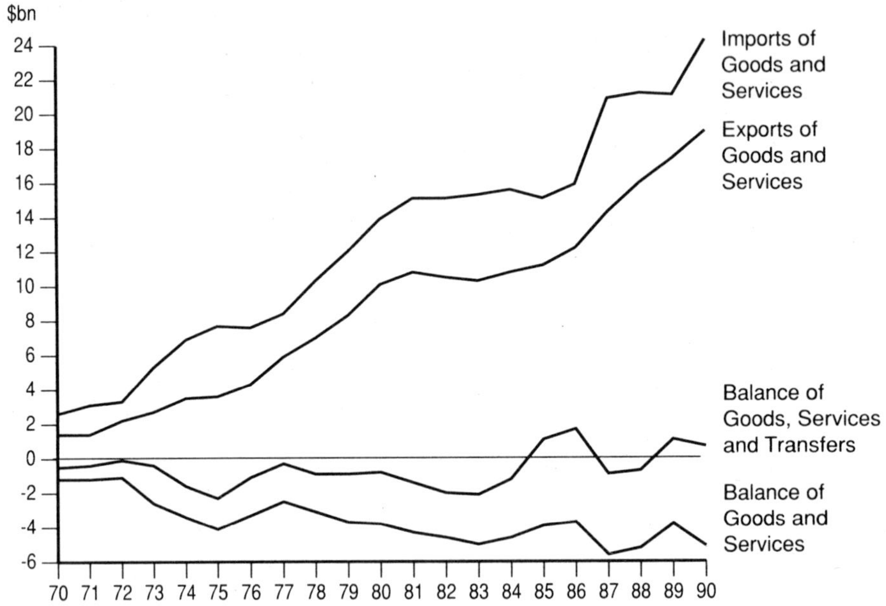

Source: Statistical Abstract of Israel, Central Bureau of Statistics
Monthly Bulletin of Statistics, Central Bureau of Statistics

growth; the trade deficit was largely financed by transfers from abroad and assistance from the U.S. government.

The 1973 war disrupted exports and increased defense imports. The war was immediately followed by the first round of international oil price rises, which pushed up the oil import bill from $93 million in 1972 to $628 million in 1975. By 1980, under the terms of the peace agreement, Israel had handed back the Sinai oil fields to Egypt and international oil prices were rising again. In 1980 oil imports reached a peak, in value terms, of nearly $1.8 billion, equal to about 8 percent of GNP. Average annual expenditure on oil imports rose from $320 million in the period 1971–1975 to $1.5 billion in 1990.

Between 1981 and 1984, in an attempt to reduce inflation, the government cut taxes on many imported goods and reduced purchase taxes, which generated a boom in domestic demand that increased imports and reduced exports. At the same time the exchange rate was held up against foreign currencies in order to reduce imported inflation. As a result Israeli exports became less competitive at a time when world trade growth was weak; imports and travel abroad by Israelis were also encouraged. The effect of these policies was a rapid worsening of the current account deficit,

TABLE 5.1
The Balance of Payments: Current and Capital Account, 1985-1990
(current dollars, millions)

	1985	1986	1987	1988	1989	1990
1. Deficit on goods and services [a]	3,882	3,729	5,627	5,173	3,768	5,086
2. Unilateral transfers	4,997	5,382	4,769	4,513	4,863	5,790
- Private	757	1,198	1,586	1,364	1,828	1,820
- Public	4,240	4,184	3,184	3,149	3,035	3,970
3. Current balance (1+2)	1,115	1,643	-858	-660	1,095	704
4. Medium & long term capital	94	538	532	-585	88	-207
5. Basic balance (3+4)	1,209	2,191	-326	-1245	1,183	497
5. Short term capital	-126	-677	839	430	-477	-336
6. Private & banking sector capital	-4	-118	0	-521	-631	-79
7. Errors and omissions	-687	-402	148	173	1,321	477
8. Change in foreign currency reserves	-392	-992	-661	1,163	1,397	-560

[a] Imports fob, Exports fob.

Source: Annual Reports 1990, Jerusalem: Bank of Israel,1991.

TABLE 5.2
The Balance of Payments: Goods and Services, 1985-1990
(current dollars, millions; imports: cif, exports: fob)

	1985	1986	1987	1988	1989	1990
Imports						
Fuel	1,510	924	1,148	1,062	1,247	1,536
Diamonds	1,168	1,598	1,901	2,613	2,861	2,895
Other goods a	4,971	6,385	7,992	8,354	8,438	10,152
Noncapital services	2,406	2,616	3,172	3,556	3,913	4,357
West Bank & Gaza	482	727	973	805	775	961
Subtotal	10,537	12,250	15,186	16,390	17,005	19,901
Capital services	2,702	2,501	2,438	2,633	2,661	2,735
Defense	1,822	1,202	2,472	2,106	1,225	1,500
Total	15,092	15,953	20,096	21,129	21,128	24,136
Exports						
Diamonds	1,263	1,664	2,059	2,746	3,027	3,054
Other goods [a]	4,739	5,211	6,078	6,912	7,625	8,496
Noncapital services	3,471	3,430	4,141	4,467	4,692	5,006
West Bank & Gaza	733	970	1,148	826	743	966
Subtotal	10,206	11,275	13,426	14,951	16,087	17,522
Capital services	1,038	850	861	1,004	1,273	1,527
Total	11,244	12,125	14,288	15,955	17,360	19,049

	1985	1986	1987	1988	1989	1990
Deficit	3,847	3,827	5,807	5,174	3,768	5,087
Deficit, excluding defense	1,995	2,625	3,335	3,068	2,543	3,587
Deficit, excluding defense and capital	331	974	1,759	1,439	1,155	2,379

[a] industry and agriculture

Sources: Annual Report 1988, Jerusalem: Bank of Israel, 1989 and Annual Report 1990, Jerusalem: Bank of Israel, 1990.

TABLE 5.3
Changes in External Conditions Facing the Israeli Economy, 1960-1985
(percent of GNP) [a]

Year	Imports of oil (1)	Total defense spending (2)	Defense spending less U.S. grants (3)	Oil and defense (4)=(1)+(3)	World trade average annual rate of growth (real terms) (5)
1960-66	1.7	na	9.0	10.7	10.0
1968-72	1.6	22.0	21.0	22.6	10.3
1974-78	5.8	29.0	18.0	23.8	4.5
1980-81	10.3	25.0	17.0	27.3	1.0
1982-83	7.9	24.5	20.0	27.9	-0.2
1984-85	7.1	24.0	16.5	23.6	5.8

[a] Years in which international oil prices rose rapidly have been excluded.

Sources: Annual Reports, Jerusalem: Bank of Israel 1961 to 1986.

which, together with the effects of the Lebanon war, resulted in a massive increase in the external debt. Rising debt servicing costs in turn worsened the deficit—a cumulative problem.

The Israeli economy has always been closely linked to the U.S. dollar (the United States is Israel's largest single trading partner), and this linkage, to what was an appreciating currency, increased the price of Israeli goods in nondollar areas. Finally, the strength of the dollar against the Western European currencies during this period further weakened Israel's competitiveness in Western Europe, its main market.

During 1984 and 1985 major improvements occurred as steps were taken to restore competitiveness, to reduce inflation, and to restrain domestic demand. Exports rose and imports fell, but in the spring of 1985 a crisis in the capital account of the balance of payments developed: Current account improvements were not happening fast enough to stem the exhaustion of the foreign exchange reserves. Emergency economic assistance from the United States, agreed to along with the economic stabilization program of July 1985, eased the situation and provided finance to cover the current account deficit. Improvements in the current account reduced the need to borrow on short-term international money markets. The dollar fell against other main currencies, and, insofar as the shekel was linked to it, Israel experienced a devaluation. Israelis, experienced in thinking in dollar terms, did not feel that there had been a depreciation of the shekel and so pressures for compensation were limited. In 1987 and 1988 the situation deteriorated as exports of goods rose but imports increased much faster. Although emergency economic aid from the United States had ended, other transfers from abroad were large enough to fund the increase in the trade deficit. The private sector has, in recent years, sold foreign currency, a reflection of its greater confidence in the shekel, something that has helped the balance of payments.

Exports

At the time of independence Israel's exports were dominated by citrus products. In 1953 agriculture accounted for 35 percent of exports, diamonds 22 percent, and industry 43 percent. From the late 1950s a range of industrial goods, of an increasingly sophisticated nature, became the largest group. By 1965 agriculture accounted for only about a quarter of export revenues and industry nearly one half.[1] Ten years later the share of agriculture had fallen to about 15 percent, that of diamonds was 30 percent and industry 55 percent.[2] Table 5.4 shows that the share of agriculture has declined still further since the mid-1980s. That of diamonds increased slightly between 1985 and 1990.

Exports in the 1980s and the beginning of the 1990s faced two conflicting trends. The first was a decline in their profitability relative to sales on domestic markets. Put simply, prices of goods on the domestic market rose more quickly than on international markets. As domestic costs rose the profits that could be obtained on foreign sales, which were subject to international competition, fell. The second trend was that international trade grew more quickly than international output. Countries traded ever larger shares of their production and so the share of exports and imports in national income rose.

This trend reflected the process of specialization. Israeli companies entered international markets to free themselves from reliance on the small and unstable domestic market. The restructuring of a number of large companies that got into severe financial difficulties resulted in the closure of less profitable production lines and further specialization. Innovative products based on local research and development, yielding relatively high profits, have become increasingly important. The best example in recent years is scientific, measuring, and related instruments, exports of which grew three times as fast as total industrial exports in current dollar terms between 1985 and 1990 (see Table 5.4).

Paradoxically, as the growth of export volumes slowed (from 7.6 percent a year in the period 1980–1985 to 6.9 percent a year in the period 1986–1989), so the share of exports in output increased.[3] In the period 1980–

TABLE 5.4
Merchandise Exports, 1985-1990
(current dollars, millions)

	1985	1986	1987	1988	1989	1990
Agriculture	468	560	609	567	527	655
Diamonds	1,263	1,665	2,059	2,746	3,027	3,054
Industry	4,359	4,709	5,544	6,348	7,143	7,890
Electrical and electronics	776	890	1,085	1,403	1,482	1,634
Textiles, clothing and leather	379	455	592	641	634	788
Chemicals, rubber and plastic	981	975	1,260	1,390	1,579	1,817
Metals ,metal products, and machinery	731	775	858	969	1,056	1,123
Transport equipment	415	556	535	462	644	581
Scientific, measuring control, optical, and photographic instruments	127	149	181	234	251	409
Total [a]	6,090	6,934	8,202	9,450	10,670	11,576

[a] Including returns

Sources: 1980 and 1985: Foreign Trade Statistics Quarterly, Central Bureau of Statistics: Vol.39, no.4, (October-December 1988), Jerusalem: Central Bureau of Statistics, March 1989; 1990: Foreign Trade Statistics Quarterly, Vol 41, no.4 (October-December 1990), Jerusalem: Central Bureau of Statistics, March 1991.

1984 exports of goods and services accounted for 33.9 percent of national income. In the period 1985–1988, they accounted for 36.6 percent.[4]

At the sectoral level the electronics industry went into international recession in 1986–1987. An international recovery occurred in 1989. The textile and clothing industries experienced a boost in demand from their main market in Western Europe in 1986–1987. They also benefitted from the strengthening of the European currencies against the dollar, which helped to lower the cost of Israeli goods there. In the period 1988–1989 European demand fell and the exchange rate of the main European importers stabilized vis-à-vis the dollar.

Exports are a major source of demand for imports. Those sectors that have higher domestic value added, therefore, contribute more to the balance of payments. The contribution of each sector is measured by its value added, that is, the share of inputs used that are locally produced. In 1953 value added in agriculture was 60 percent, in diamonds 14 percent, and in the rest of industry 35 percent. By 1965 the share in agriculture had reached 80 percent, in diamonds 23 percent, and in industry 59 percent. There has been relatively little change since then.

In 1972 exports of services, other than capital, came to $745 million. Of this, $212 million was from tourism. In 1989 these items came to $4.9 billion and $1.5 billion respectively. Tourist revenues grew by 50 percent between 1986 and 1989 despite terrorism and the Palestinian uprising. In 1989, 1.2 million tourists visited Israel, 14 percent fewer than the 1987 peak. The Gulf crisis in 1990 and the war in 1991 resulted in further large declines.

Exports of freight and transportation services reflect the high cost of exporting from Israel to practically all its markets; very little trade is done with neighboring countries. In 1989 exports of transport services came to $1.8 billion, of which $440 million was for the import of goods to Israel by Israeli air and maritime transport.

Imports

In 1972, the last year of fast economic growth, consumer goods accounted for 11.6 percent of imports and production goods 47.6 percent (of which fuel took 4.9 percent). Diamonds were 16 percent of imports and investment goods 24.8 percent. By 1985 the share of consumer goods had fallen, as had that of investment goods. The increase in the share of production goods reflected the increased price of oil and the increasing importance of exports, which had a large import content. The most dramatic change was in the share of production goods, which rose by over 20 percent, mainly as a result of the increase in international oil prices: They increased more slowly than industrial exports. Exports of metal products and electrical and electronic goods, where most of these production imports were used, rose by 570 percent from 1972 to 1985, resulting from increased efficiency in their use and greater value added in exports.

Table 5.5 shows the changes in imports between 1985 and 1990. Between 1985 and 1989 there was a further fall in the share of investment goods, reflecting the recession that developed in 1988 and deepened in 1989. There was also a fall in the share of consumer goods, also due to the recession. The partial recovery of the economy in 1990, which was based on increased construction of housing for immigrants, resulted in a rise in the share of investment goods.

The slump of recent years caused a slowdown in the growth of import volumes from 15 percent a year in the period 1986–1987 to minus 2 percent in the period 1988–1989. This decline was a considerable turnaround in view of the internationalization process described above. It took place against a background of higher taxes on imports. In 1980 the average tax rate on imports was 8 percent; in 1986 it was 16 percent. By 1989 it was 11 percent. The reduction in customs duties on European Community (EC) imports, which was part of the trade agreement with that bloc, was more than offset by increases in purchase taxes and by the increased weight of very highly taxed consumer durables in the total import bill between 1980 and 1986.[5]

The Geographic Distribution of Israel's Trade

There are considerable imbalances in the distribution of Israel's trade. The main one is the deficit with the EC and with other European countries: It exceeds the total deficit. Israel is, therefore, in surplus in its trade with non–Western European countries.

Table 5.6 shows the geographic breakdown of exports and imports of goods. The European Community and the European Free Trade Area are together Israel's largest market and account for about 40 percent of sales. These are the geographically closest markets to Israel, and cultural links as well as the industrial free trade area with the EC have played important roles in the development of exports. The EC is, however, a much more protected market for high-technology exports than the United States. The relatively fast growth of high-technology exports has been a result of sales in the United States rather than in Europe and is a major reason for the fall since 1980 in the share of total exports going to the EC and the increase in that going to the United States.

Between 1985 and 1990 Western Europe increased its share of Israel's imports by 5 percent, while the share of the United States fell by 3 percent. This change reflected in part the strength of the dollar during much of the

TABLE 5.5
Merchandise Imports, 1985-1990
(excluding direct defense; current dollars, percent)

	1985	%	1989	%	1990	%
Private consumption	621	7.6	1,326	10.4	1,599	10.4
Investment	1,414	17.2	1,614	12.6	2,229	14.6
Production	6,162	75.2	9,840	77.0	11,486	75.0
Total	8,197	100.0	12,780	100.0	15,314	100.0

Sources: Annual Report 1988, Jerusalem: 1989 Annual Report 1990, Jerusalem: Bank of Israel 1991.

TABLE 5.6
Geographic Breakdown of Israel's Trade, 1980-1990
(current dollars, percent)

Region	1980	1985	1990
Exports			
Europe	52.2	37.2	40.0
EC	41.2	31.2	34.0
North America [a]	18.2	35.4	29.6
U.S.A.	17.2	34.2	28.7
Central & South America	2.9	2.3	2.4
Asia	11.0	8.6	15.2
Africa	3.4	1.7	1.2
Oceania	1.0	1.0	0.8
Other [b]	11.2	13.8	10.8
Total	100.0	100.0	100.0
Imports			
Europe	46.0	54.4	62.0
EC	34.3	44.9	49.3
North America [a]	22.0	21.5	18.8
U.S.A.	20.5	20.2	17.8
Central & South America	1.5	1.3	1.1
Asia	2.5	3.4	6.8
Africa	1.7	2.2	1.8
Oceania	0.5	0.6	0.2
Other [c]	27.3	16.6	9.3
Total	100.0	100.0	100.0

[a] 1980-1985: USA, Canada & Mexico. 1990: USA & Canada.
[b] Mainly military exports
[c] Mainly oil

Sources: 1980-1985: Foreign Trade Statistics Quarterly, Vol. 37 no.4 (October-December 1986), Jerusalem: Central Bureau of Statistics, and Foreign Trade Statistics Quarterly, Vol.39, no.4 (October-December 1988). 1990: Foreign Trade Statistics Quarterly: Import-Export Commodities, Jerusalem: Central Bureau of Statistics, April-June 1991, Vol. 42 no.4, September 1991.

period and the natural tendency to import from geographically close regions. The EC accounts for about 85 percent of Israel's trade with Europe.

Israel has a larger trade deficit with the EC than its total trade deficit due to two factors: a deficit on trade in industrial goods and the fact that much of Israel's fuel and diamonds is bought on EC markets. The deficit with Europe is also partly the result of trade-diverting import duties and quotas in Israel. In order to minimize cheap imports from the Far East and thus protect local industry, duties and quotas are imposed on imports from those countries. As a result more expensive alternatives are imported from Europe (see "Protectionism" below).

Financing the Import Surplus

The annual deficit on goods and services averaged $4.4 billion from 1980 to 1985. In the period 1986 to 1989 it increased to an average of $4.6 billion a year, despite the fall in the international price of oil. Table 5.1 shows how the deficit was financed. In 1985 there was, for the first time, a surplus on the current account including transfers (United States aid, other official inflows, and private transfers). This surplus represented a huge change and resulted from a decline in the deficit on goods and services of $1 billion in 1984 and 1985 and a rise in transfers of $2.2 billion, all of which was due to increased U.S. government grants.

The pattern was broadly similar in 1986, but the following year brought a major deterioration. The deficit on goods and services increased by $2 billion to over $5 billion and remained at that level in 1988. United States aid fell in 1986 and 1987 compared with the previous two years, and as a result the current account went into deficit. The turnaround on the current account between 1986 and 1987 was nearly $2.5 billion. In 1989 the domestic recession deepened and the deficit on goods and services was reduced by $1.5 billion. Once again transfer payments more than covered the deficit, which resulted in a surplus on the current account.

Israel has another source of preferential finance from abroad: transfers by individuals. These rose by 140 percent, in current dollar terms, between 1985 and 1989. Improvements in the balance of payments permitted the economy to reduce its use of external loans. The United States converted all of its assistance to grants in 1985, and in that year Israel became a net repayer of long- and short-term loans.

External Debt

External debt provides resources not produced by domestic activity or foreign grants: It can assist in increasing the rate of economic growth. For the debt to play a positive role, the government has to adjust the scale and composition of interest and capital repayments to its payment capacity. The key to successful borrowing lies in maintaining a healthy reputation on international markets so that the economy can borrow abroad when necessary. Debt should, therefore, be used in ways that, inter alia, provide the means for its repayment. In macroeconomic terms this strategy means increasing investment rather than consumption.

Debt is usually discussed in relative terms, thus providing an indication of the burden of financing and the scale of the debt in relation to the economy and its exports. Israel's debt is denominated in foreign currency while its national income is in shekels. The relationship between the two is affected by the exchange rate and by the rate of inflation. It is, therefore, most useful for general analysis to concentrate on the ratios of debt servicing to exports.

The ratio of debt servicing to exports is the key measure of the pressure of debt in the economy because exports, along with capital inflows, provide the means to repay the debt. This ability to service the debt is a function of the size of the debt, its composition, the level of interest rates, and the volume of exports.

In the years up to 1985 short-term borrowing, which was the most expensive in terms of high and often floating interest rates, increased. As can be seen in Table 5.7, net interest and capital repayments on the foreign debt as a share of exports of goods and services (excluding exports of capital services) rose from 23 percent in 1981 to a peak of 30 percent in 1985. In 1989 they accounted for 19 percent.

In 1985, 64 percent of the debt belonged to the public sector, mainly the central government. After a fall to 58 percent in 1987, it rose to 64 percent in 1989. The rise in 1989 was due to increased public sector demand and the recession in the private sector. Despite the secular rise in the burden until the mid-1980s, Israel always met its external financial obligations. The net debt, which is the amount owed to foreigners minus financial assets abroad, totalled $15.5 billion at the end September 1991.

Loans from the U.S. government have been important and have been extended in various forms for different purposes since the foundation of the state. Between 1952 and 1961 total U.S. grants and loans came to $561 million; from 1962 to 1972 they totalled $1.6 billion and from 1973 to 1985 about $27 billion. Between 1986 and 1988 they totalled $10.5 billion, most of which consisted of grants. The $12 billion of loans form the largest component of the external debt.

Much of the debt was, therefore, on favorable terms: Fixed interest rates were significantly lower than market ones. The sale of Israeli government bonds, mainly in the United States, was another way of securing preferential finance. These bonds had relatively low interest rates: Their sales depended on the willingness of the purchaser to forgo an element of his

TABLE 5.7
External Debt and Servicing Costs, 1980-1990
(current dollars, billions)

	1980	1981	1982	1983	1984	1985	1986	1987	1988	1989	1990
Net Debt [a]	11.6	13.3	15.6	18.3	18.9	18.4	18.2	18.2	18.8	16.4	15.6
1.Interest payments as percent of exports [b]	11	9	12	13	18	17	14	11	11	8	6
2.Capital repayments as percent of exports [b]	10	14	14	13	12	13	15	14	13	11	11
3.Total debt servicing as percent of exports (3=1+2)	21	23	26	26	30	29	29	25	24	19	17

[a] Net liabilities equal gross liabilities minus assets.
[b] Excluding exports of capital services.

Sources: 1980-1983: Annual Report 1984, Jerusalem: Bank of Israel, 1985: 1984: Annual Report 1986, Jerusalem: Bank of Israel, 1987; 1985-1989: Annual Report 1989, Jerusalem: Bank of Israel, 1989.1990: Annual Report 1990, Jerusalem: Bank of Israel, 1991.

return in order to contribute toward the development of the Israeli economy. They were, and are, very long term (fifteen to twenty-nine years) but can be redeemed prematurely with ninety days notice, in Israeli currency, by various categories of purchasers. The pressure of repayment has been eased by giving many purchasers the right to trade in their bonds for new issues. Some purchases can be considered as partial substitutes for donations to the United Jewish Appeal, through which the U.S. Jewish community makes large contributions to Israel.

Foreign Trade Policy

Liberalization in the 1960s

In the 1960s the economy was opened to international competition in a fundamental way. The consequences included an expansion of the foreign trade sector, increased competitiveness in the economy, and greater industrial production.[6]

Between 1951 and 1958 the rise in exports was mainly the result of increased production of citrus products and sales of diamonds. From 1958, manufactured exports (excluding diamonds) increased rapidly. During the 1960s import substitution became less important. In 1962 a new economic policy was announced, including a devaluation designed to improve the balance of payments and eliminate multiple exchange rates. Some moves were made toward fiscal protection away from administrative controls (except in agriculture), but the policy failed to improve the balance of payments because it was not accompanied by a reduction in domestic demand. Only in 1965 did the government act to stimulate exports when it realized that devaluation alone would not have the desired effect.

The government has, since the 1960s, encouraged the development of exports by direct financial aid and through assistance in establishing new enterprises that commit themselves to export. The Ministry of Industry and Trade has at times encouraged mergers when higher exports, more competition, and greater efficiency were the expected results.[7] The government also negotiated trade agreements abroad, designed to increase exports.

The European Community–Israel Trade Agreements

Negotiations began in 1962 on a five-year preferential trade agreement between Israel and the EC that was signed in 1970. It provided for a 50 percent reduction in the EC's common external tariff on 70 percent of Israeli industrial exports and on 40 percent of citrus exports. A second, more comprehensive agreement was signed in 1975. This agreement provided for the free entry of all manufactured goods from Israel to the then-expanded EC, with the exception of some textile and chemical items that were subject to duty-free quotas. Implementation began in July 1977.

On the other side, those EC goods not having equivalents produced in Israel were until 1979 subject to reduced tariffs. Infant industry protection, in the form of low tariff barriers, was permitted until 1989. On commodities having equivalents produced in Israel, tariffs were reduced from 1978 and were due to be ended by 1984 but were extended to 1989 under the terms of the agreement. A 60 percent reduction in Israeli customs duties on imports from the EC took place on January 1, 1987, and they were abolished at the end of 1989.

Duties on Israeli agricultural commodities were reduced substantially but not abolished. The agreement also contained protocols on cooperation in finance, science, patents, the promotion of Israeli exports to the EC, agriculture, fishing, and private investment.

The U.S.-Israel Free Trade Agreement

Negotiations began in 1983 on an agreement to mutually reduce and then eliminate tariff and nontariff barriers on trade between the United States and Israel. In April of that year a free trade agreement (FTA) was signed by the two countries, with reductions in tariffs to start in July 1985 and be completed by January 1995. This was the first comprehensive bilateral trade agreement signed by the United States.

The agreement prevents Israel from imposing infant industry protection after 1995 and restricts temporary measures, such as increased import duties and import deposits, to 150 days duration. This measure was a limit on Israel's rights under the General Agreement on Tariffs and Trade (GATT). Performance requirements for assistance to foreign investors are excluded and export subsidies were to be abolished by 1991. The latter did not happen in 1991.

Some estimates of the effects of these and other provisions of the agreement on the Israeli economy suggest that they will be very small. Exports to the United States could, according to these calculations, increase by 1 percent a year, but U.S. exports to Israel may grow more quickly. Reduction of Israeli tariffs on U.S. exports to the levels imposed on EC exports in 1985 would result in a 2 percent increase; their elimination would result in a 8.4 percent rise.[8]

If the "hidden" tariff that Israel imposes were included in the calculations, the increase in U.S. exports under these two cases would be 12.1 percent and 18.4 percent, respectively. (See "Protectionism" below.) After the implementation of the Israel-EC agreement, Israel took compensating measures to preserve the relative prices for a number of key sectors where import tariffs were reduced or eliminated. This move could happen under the FTA, thus reducing the expansion of U.S. imports.

The difference between the gains for the two countries is a result of the low level of U.S. tariffs imposed on Israeli exports before the FTA was signed and the high level of Israeli tariffs on U.S. imports. Many Israeli exports were free of duty under the most favored nation provision of GATT and under the Generalized System of Preferences.

The advantage of the agreement, from Israel's point of view, is that it makes the current low levels and later zero levels of U.S. tariffs permanent. Of the $1.25 billion exported by Israel to the United States in 1983, only $887 million was dutiable; the duties paid came to 11 percent. Of the $1.54 billion of U.S. exports to Israel in 1982, $598 million were dutiable, and duties paid came to 12 percent. The hidden tariff came to $130.6 million and was paid on all imports.[9]

Israel also has a military agreement with the United States entitled the Memo of Understanding. It was signed in 1979 and in 1984 was renewed for a further five years with modifications and additions. The agreement gives Israeli companies the right to bid for U.S. military contracts in the same way that NATO countries are permitted. Originally, Israeli military exports of $200 million were envisaged but sales now total about $100 million, having increased from $45 million in 1982. These are mainly contracts won by Israel's largest defense suppliers. A memo on Israel's participation in the Strategic Defense Initiative has also been signed by the two governments.

Protectionism

Despite the FTA, the agreement with the EC, and membership in GATT, Israel's economy is highly protected. There are duties and, until September 1, 1991, there were quotas on imports from countries other than the United States and the EC. There is also a 1 percent foreign exchange tax, a 2 percent tax on all imports, an addition-to-purchase tax applicable to imports rather than domestically produced goods (known by its Hebrew acronym "Tama"), and an exemptions-from-purchase tax for certain categories of locally made goods. Nontariff barriers include quotas on imports of some consumer goods from cheap sources of supply, prohibitions on the imports of some items, and special standards designed to help local producers. Taxes on imports have to be paid immediately upon arrival in the country; those on locally made goods can be paid up to three months after sales are made. Israel is not unique in adopting measures to protect local production but the array of them and their strength are formidable. Domestic consumers were further affected by the practice, until September 1, 1991, of licensing importers, even when a quota limited the amount that could be brought into the country. This monopolization further reduced competition and was another source of high prices and costs.

In 1986, according to an official definition, only 31 percent of imports were defined as competitive. Competitive imports include those goods on which the rate of taxation (excluding purchase tax) exceeded 20 percent, assuming that the tax was intended to defend local production. It also included goods for which local production accounted for more than 20 percent of total sources (local production and imports). The figure was 40.9 percent when fuel imports were excluded. Of consumer goods imports, 56.3 percent were competitive, but only 27.3 percent of production goods (including fuel) and 31.1 percent of investment goods were competitive.

There is evidence that protectionism increased in the 1980s, in contrast to the 1970s. According to the Bank of Israel, the price of Israeli-made goods was on average 30 percent higher than that of imports. During the 1970s Israeli prices fell by 15 percent in comparison with those of imports, the result of increased import duties and administrative controls on goods coming into the country. For industries that were highly cartelized or were monopolies, the difference exceeded 30 percent.[10]

Purchase tax is paid on local production but often at different effective rates because of the system of hidden tariffs. An extreme example is that of carpets: The total tax on an imported carpet in 1988 was 155 percent, while that on a locally made product was about 25 percent. Total taxes paid on imports (excluding value-added tax) doubled from 8 percent to 16 percent between 1980 and 1986. This increase was despite trade agreements with the EC and the United States that brought reductions in customs duties and further reductions in 1981 and 1982. Purchase taxes on imports were increased to compensate for the customs reductions, and demand for relatively highly taxed imports, such as automobiles, rose sharply.[11]

A major criticism of the trade agreements that Israel has signed is that they encourage imports from high cost areas. For example, clothing imports from the EC are not subject to import duties but those from Southeast Asia are subject to duties and even to quotas. This policy helps to protect domestic industry from competition with cheaper producers and forces Israeli consumers to pay higher prices. Losses of foreign exchange because of this trade diversion effect have been estimated at $200 million.[12]

Exchange Rate Policy

The effectiveness of devaluations in improving the balance of payments weakened in the 1960s. Until 1962 there had been a long lag between the devaluation and a compensating increase in prices. The exchange rate adjustment was, therefore, effective for several years. After the 1962 devaluation the lag in the movement of domestic prices was much shorter, and they caught up by mid-1965. In the summer of 1970, prices rose soon after the devaluation of that August, although there were inflationary pressures before the exchange rate move.[13]

An important reason why the adjustment of prices to a devaluation accelerated was that foreign exchange and later foreign exchange–denominated assets played an increasingly important role in the economy. The value of these assets rose in domestic currency terms when a devaluation occurred: In this way, devaluations stimulated consumption and inflationary demand pressures.

The government sold foreign exchange to the public in order to fund its budget deficit. Between 1980 and 1982 foreign currency sales to the public covered an average of 27.7 percent of the deficit. In 1983 and 1984 the share rose to 82 percent, and in 1985, as a result of the stabilization program, it fell back to 45 percent. Between 1980 and 1985 a total of $7.8 billion was added to the public's holdings of foreign currency in this way.

In the mid-1980s influential economic analysis in Israel drew attention to the link between the inflation rate and the balance of payments.[14] In 1974, 1979, and 1983 balance-of-payments crises precipitated accelerated inflation. The 1977 and 1984 devaluations designed to improve the balance of payments were accompanied by "price shocks": large reductions in subsidies. These decreases in subsidies were aimed at reducing the size of the government deficit more quickly than government spending cuts could and also at lowering total demand. In a system of near complete linkage, subsidy reductions, resulting in price rises, caused compensating wage rises and thus cost and price rises. Eventually the government found that it was having to pay more to its own employees and was, therefore, not able to reduce its deficit. The exchange rate continued to be devalued in order to compensate for domestic inflation with little or no real depreciation being achieved.

Until 1975 official policy stated that each devaluation that occurred would be the last one. In 1975 the crawling peg system was introduced, and by changing the rate every day the exchange rate ceased to be an anchor in the price system.

In the early 1980s the exchange rate ceased to have a role as a weapon of economic control; it had become a cog in the inflationary process. During the years 1981 to 1983 it was artificially held up, causing a real appreciation in the external value of the shekel. The consequences for the balance of payments were severe, and the policy was abandoned in the autumn of 1983. The shekel was devalued and allowed to float down against the dollar and other foreign currencies. In the mid-1980s the idea that a fixed exchange rate could help to provide an anchor of stability was developed. It represented a radical departure from the practice of the previous ten years. The idea that domestic cost cutting should be pursued rather than devaluation was not, however, new. It had been advocated in the 1950s and 1960s when inflation was much lower.[15]

In July 1985, after an 18 percent devaluation, the shekel was fixed against the dollar. Prices in the economy were frozen, and as the European currencies increased in value against the dollar, importers of goods from those countries found themselves paying more but only being able to charge according to the exchange rate on July 1, 1985. This situation caused problems of supply, and at the end of the year price rises were permitted on imported goods.

In July 1986 the shekel was linked to a basket of the currencies of Israel's major trading partners; the aim of the change was to reduce the imported inflation that resulted from tying the shekel to the weaker dollar.[16] The implied preference was to further reduce inflation rather than directly assist exporters, who hoped for a devaluation to compensate them for domestic inflation, a cumulative problem.

In January 1987 a package of measures designed to improve the balance of payments was introduced. It included a 10 percent devaluation of the shekel, reductions in subsidies, delay in the payment of a cost-of-living increase due to workers, continuation of price controls, and a cut in the employers' contribution to national insurance. Reductions were made in the state budget and lower taxes for firms and individuals were proposed. The government agreed to continue its reforms of the capital market, although shortly afterward the 1987/88 budget was issued with a planned deficit.

These measures were similar in kind to the July 1985 package but were much smaller in scale and, therefore, less radical. The loss of export competitiveness between July 1985 and January 1987 resulted from inflation combined with a virtually fixed dollar-shekel exchange rate. At the end of 1988 devaluations totalling 13 percent were implemented. Subsidies to consumers were reduced and a cost-of-living agreement providing for only partial compensation for wage earners was agreed to. In June 1989 there was another, 5 percent, devaluation.

Economic Relations with the Arabs

Trade with the Administered Territories

Trade between Israel and the West Bank and Gaza, captured by Israel in the 1967 war (the "territories"), increased substantially over the last twenty-one years. Imports of services are almost entirely of labor services used in the building, tourist, and other service industries. As a result of the 1984–1985 recession, demand for labor in the building industry fell, causing a reduction in wages earned. Israeli exports of goods increased sharply until 1983; since then, demand in the territories has fallen because incomes earned by Arab workers have declined and so have remittances from Arab oil states. These factors taken together led to a near doubling of Israel's surplus with the territories.

The gain to Israel from this relationship is not only reflected in the balance of payments. Mainly unskilled or semiskilled workers commute into Israel on a daily basis, many without fixed employment. The number involved has grown from a few thousand in 1967–1968 to nearly 100,000 in 1986. Workers from the territories constitute about 6 percent of the labor force but up to 25 percent in construction. Skilled labor emigrated from the territories to the oil-rich Arab states. Those who have returned since the slump in the international price of oil have been unable or unwilling to fit into the Israeli labor market.

The supply of labor from the territories has reduced the rate of technological development in the construction industry and some other parts of the economy. However, the supply of relatively cheap labor in flexible quantities after 1967 enabled the economy, particularly the construction sector, to grow rapidly, with only limited inflationary pressures.

The areas occupied in 1967, including the Golan, have provided land for Israeli settlements. Increased water supplies and a limited number of other resources also became available to Israel in 1967, but the overall value to the economy of the territories is a matter of deep controversy.

Many critics of Israel point to the relationship as classically colonialist and exploitative. Many in Israel feel that the political and security costs to Israel are far greater than any possible economic gains. Few would disagree with the view that the West Bank has not been developed to its potential because of the policies pursued by Jordan until 1967 and Israel since then. The fact that many skilled workers found employment in the Arab oil states and many unskilled ones worked in Israel has also been detrimental to the development of the region.

The Palestinian Uprising and Its Economic Effects

From November 1987 into the early 1990s, riots and serious disturbances have continued throughout the West Bank and Gaza. These events have had a much larger effect on the economies of those areas than on that of Israel. The economic systems of the territories and Israel have become closely interlinked but a huge imbalance exists between them: Israel's GNP is about 13 times as large; on a per capita basis the gap is even larger. The uprising reduced the level of tourism from abroad, probably by about 15 percent, or $140 million, equivalent to 0.4 percent of GNP in 1988. The withdrawal of Arab labor was about 25 percent, mainly affecting construction and to a lesser extent agriculture. The loss of output was similar to that in tourism. The income losses suffered in the territories as a result of falling earnings from employment in Israel were proportionately much larger, which reduced the demand for Israeli goods and services. Exports of Israeli goods fell from $928 million in 1987 to $600 million in 1989. At the same time Israelis bought less from the territories. The net loss to Israel was about 0.3 percent of GNP. A further cost to Israel has been the doubling of army reserve duty, which resulted in a loss of output of between 0.3 percent and 0.4 percent of GNP. The total cost was, therefore, equal to between 1 percent and 1.5 percent of GNP in 1988 and 1989.

The Arab Boycott

In 1946 the Arab League decided on a boycott of the Jewish community in Mandatory Palestine. Since 1948 the league's activities have been directed against foreign companies trading with Israel. No Arab states, except Egypt, officially trade with Israel; in fact, Israeli goods cross the River Jordan cease-fire line to many Arab countries. Since 1982 there has been trade with Lebanon.

There are three aspects to the boycott. The primary boycott is that of Israel by the Arab states, except Egypt. The secondary boycott seeks to prevent relations from developing between Arabs and foreign companies that have, as the Central Office for the Boycott of Israel, in Damascus, calls it, "prohibited" links with Israel in terms of trade or investment. Finally, the tertiary boycott seeks to prevent non-Arab firms from dealing with blacklisted ones. The boycott has had mixed success: When it is convenient, Arab states have ignored it. It has, however, helped to discourage trade with and investment in Israel.

Economic Relations with Egypt

The most important item in the Israel-Egypt economic relationship is the sale of Egyptian oil to Israel under the terms of the peace treaty between the two countries. Israel does not disclose figures on its oil imports, and they are excluded from statistics on the geographic distribution of imports. A contract for 2 million tons of crude oil was negotiated at the end of 1986, which accounted for about 30 percent of Israeli consumption.[17] Israeli exports to Egypt came to $4.5 million in 1989 and nonoil imports from Egypt totalled $4.9 million.

Although a large number of Israelis have visited Egypt, the number of Egyptians visiting Israel has been very small. Most of the tourist trade and border crossings have been accounted for by Israelis, residents of the West Bank and Gaza, as well as citizens of other countries.[18]

Conclusion

Israel has chronic balance-of-payments problems. The balance of payments has been the catalyst for economic policy changes because policy makers have always feared the consequences of running out of foreign exchange or an inability to secure loans abroad.

Between 1985 and 1990, there was an improvement in the current account, with the emergence of small surpluses. This development was made possible by additional emergency aid from the United States except in 1989 when there was a surplus without extra assistance, largely due to the recession. All of these changes helped to reduce the level of external debt, which in turn will ease the financing burden in future years. As long as the defense burden remains high, however, there are likely to be balance-of-payments problems.

The central failures of economic policy in the international sector have been twofold. First, the government has not been able to effect a real devaluation for long enough to improve the balance of payments without generating inflationary pressures. Second, it has failed to substantially liberalize foreign trade. These shortcomings have helped to prevent structural changes vital for the development of the economy.

Notes

1. N. Halevi and R. Klinov-Malul, *The Economic Development of Israel* (New York: Praeger and Bank of Israel, 1968), p. 148.
2. *Annual Report 1976* (Jerusalem: Bank of Israel, 1977). In Hebrew.
3. *Annual Report 1989* (Jerusalem: Bank of Israel, 1990). In Hebrew.
4. *Annual Report 1988* (Jerusalem: Bank of Israel, 1989). In Hebrew.
5. *Annual Report 1989* (Jerusalem: Bank of Israel, 1990). In Hebrew.
6. A. Bregman, *Industry and Industrial Policy in Israel 1965–85* (Jerusalem: Bank of Israel, 1986). In Hebrew.
7. R. Pomfret, *Trade Policies and Industrialization in a Small Country: The Case of Israel* (Tubingen: JCB Mohr/Paul Siebeck, 1976).
8. J. Pelzman, *The Impact of the US-Israel Free Trade Area Agreement on Israeli Trade and Employment* (Jerusalem: Falk Institute, 1985).
9. Ibid.
10. *Ha'aretz* (Tel Aviv), 26 March 1990. In Hebrew.
11. *Annual Report 1989* (Jerusalem: Bank of Israel, 1990).
12. *Ha'aretz*, 6 October 1989. In Hebrew.
13. M. Michaeli, *Foreign Trade Regimes and Economic Development: Israel* (New York: National Bureau for Economic Research, Columbia University Press, 1975).

14. N. Liviatan and S. Piterman, *Accelerating Inflation and Balance of Payments Crises 1973–84* (Jerusalem: Bank of Israel Discussion Paper, 1984).

15. A. Lerner, "Stabilization and Economic Independence," *Economic Quarterly*, vol. 5–6 (Tel Aviv: October 1954). In Hebrew.

16. M. Bruno, *Israel's Stabilization: The End of the Lost Decade* (Jerusalem: Falk Institute Conference Paper, 1986).

17. *Davar* (Tel Aviv), 22 December 1986. In Hebrew.

18. *Tourism and Hotel Service Statistics Quarterly* (Jerusalem: Central Bureau of Statistics and Ministry of Tourism, 1991), vol. 19, no. 3.

6

The Capital Market and Financial Sector

The extensive involvement of the government in Israel's capital market has meant significant deviations from the free market model, with important consequences for the economy. The public supplies funds to those who need credit through its deposits in the banks, savings schemes, mutual funds, and social and life insurance. Savings schemes are operated by the banks and are of varied duration; some are linked to the exchange rate for foreign currencies and others to the consumer price index. Social insurance funds, dominated by those of the Histadrut, cover sickness pay, convalescence, holiday leave, and old age pensions. The social insurance funds act as intermediaries, mobilizing resources, allocating a small share to themselves each year, and passing the balance on to other financial intermediaries. There are tax incentives designed to encourage employees to contribute to these programs. Most of the funds are ultimately invested in government bonds because only the state has been able to offer linkage to the consumer price index, which made the investment virtually risk free because there was no chance of a real fall in value. In 1990 the government required financial institutions to invest large proportions of their funds in bonds that it issued: Pension funds managers had to invest 93 percent of their resources in official bonds; compensation funds and advanced training funds, 72 percent.[1] These quotas had been even higher in previous years. The government used the funds to cover its budget deficit and to finance its debt repayment program.

The Role of the Government

Israel has traditionally had a high savings ratio, partly because the government has provided strong incentives to save. A large proportion of these savings have, however, been used by the government to finance its deficit, in turn permitting high levels of public investment, consumption, and transfers.

The extent of government domination of the capital market increased sharply between the mid-1970s and the mid-1980s as the budget deficit rose. In 1976, 58 percent of funds raised (through state loans, bonds, and issuing shares) in the economy were accounted for by the public sector. In 1985 its share reached a peak of 96 percent, declining to 86.2 percent in 1986.[2] Behind the deficit lay a huge national debt. One-third of it was external, foreign currency denominated, and owed to foreigners; two-thirds was internal, in shekels, and owed to Israelis. (The external debt is examined in Chapter 5.)

The debt rose rapidly from about 123 percent of gross domestic product (GDP) in the late 1970s to 145 percent at the end of 1985. This increase was because the government borrowed expensively, while it sold index-linked assets and lent cheaply. As inflation accelerated, the value of its assets fell and those of its obligations rose. In 1983 the bank share arrangement (see "The Bank Share Collapse of 1983 and Its Aftermath" below) increased the debt ratio by 11.5 percent at a stroke. The gap was met by increased borrowing and, in 1985, a large increase in taxation, which broke the debt spiral. By the end of 1988 the ratio had fallen to 121 percent.

The government deficit and the way in which it was financed were the main factors behind the growth of financial asset holdings. Between 1976 and 1985 they increased by 63 percent in real terms; most of this growth occurred prior to 1983.

In 1983 and 1984 the government, through the Bank of Israel, sold large amounts of foreign currency to the public, as the latter lost faith in the state's ability to meet interest payments and repay capital. During the years of high inflation, the printing of money was relatively unimportant; the public did not want to increase its holdings of cash or retain them for longer than absolutely necessary. Indexed bonds of varying degrees of liquidity were issued and these, together with sales of foreign currency, were the main ways in which the deficits were financed. Sales of foreign currency to the public increased external debt and interest payments abroad, thus aggravating balance-of-payments problems.

The linking of bonds to the consumer price index or to the dollar started in 1955, and it has been both a cause and result of the government's domination of the capital market.[3] Linked bonds were simple and cheap to issue and administer. Rapid growth in the use of foreign-linked bonds was experienced in the early 1980s. This kind of linkage had the advantage of daily exchange-rate quotations rather than the monthly announcements of the rise in consumer prices. As inflation accelerated, demand and time deposits, whose values were linked to changes in the exchange rate of the shekel, became increasingly attractive. Purchases of foreign currency and foreign currency–linked assets reflected the public's anticipation of a devaluation. Net financial obligations in foreign currency as a share of total financial wealth increased from 13.2 percent in 1981 to 34.4 percent in the second quarter of 1985. The purchase of foreign currency became a key mechanism linking the budget and balance-of-payments deficits, as was shown in Chapter 2. By reducing inflation and the level of uncertainty in financial markets, the July 1985 stabilization program reduced the share of foreign currency assets in total financial wealth in the third quarter of that year to 28.1 percent.

In 1989 new, six-year, bonds were issued without linkage for the first year; this partial removal of linkage was an indication of the limited progress that has been made in restoring faith in capital markets. The degree of linkage has varied, as has the tax treatment of interest on these bonds.

The linked nature of virtually all of the debt meant that inflation could not erode its real value; thus, the government did not benefit from an inflation tax. Conversely, due to what has been described as one of the most sophisticated systems of linkage in the world, the government was able to raise funds in difficult circumstances.[4] The scale of the problem is shown by looking at how expenditure on the debt rose.

In 1970 the government spent nearly $543 million repaying debt, equal to about 10 percent of gross national product (GNP). Fifty-seven percent went to interest payments. In 1975 total debt repayments had risen to nearly $1.7 billion, or 13.7 percent of GNP. The effects of the Yom Kippur War and the rise in international oil prices were felt by 1980, when total debt payments came to $5.8 billion. In 1984 a peak of about $20 billion was allocated to debt repayment. By 1988 this amount had fallen to $15.4 billion, including $4 billion to redeem bank shares under the 1983 bank share arrangement (see "The Bank Share Collapse of 1983 and Its Aftermath" below). Interest payments were budgeted to account for 29 percent of the total compared with a peak of 63.7 percent in the period 1981–1983.[5] The total allocation has fallen since 1988, but the share of interest has risen. The reduction in the budget deficit since 1985 permitted a fall in borrowing, which enabled the government to offer lower interest rates on the bonds that it issued and to issue them for longer durations. The effect has been to lower interest costs in the budget and thus reduce the borrowing requirements. In 1985 the government redeemed 2 percent of the bonds that had matured and recycled the remaining 98 percent by issuing new ones. In 1986 and 1987 it was able to redeem 16 percent.

The government's role in the capital market has been the main cause of a high level of savings in the economy. These savings were, up to 1985, increasingly used to finance the government's current expenditure rather than investment. It also controlled private sector bond issues by placing overall limits on the amounts that could be raised by firms. The reduction in the government deficit and liberalization of capital market regulations resulted in an increase in private sector issues from 1985. They accounted for 2 percent of investment in 1983–1985 and 11 percent in 1986–1987.[6]

There was an improvement in conditions in the capital market between 1985 and 1987 as a result of reduced government intervention, mainly due to the fall in the budget deficit and that of the level of debt expenditure. There were also reforms in the money market in the form of reduced liquidity ratios imposed on the commercial banks. Foreign exchange regulations have been eased somewhat. These changes were not accompanied by privatization, as promised by the government, and the government has still not sold its shares in the banks. As a result the liberalization has been limited, and the private sector, much of which went into recession in the period 1988–1989, was unable to make greater use of the capital markets.[7]

The Bank of Israel and Monetary Policy

The government's activities in the capital market are carried out with the support of the Bank of Israel through its monetary policy. The central bank has a large number of functions in the capital markets and the economy as a whole. It directs credit on behalf of the government, raises funds for the state, controls the foreign exchange reserves, manages the exchange rate, and administers exchange control regulations. The central bank supervises the activities of banks and financial institutions, advises the government on economic and financial matters, and conducts research. It is also responsible for issuing and controlling the currency and coordinating with international bodies such as the International Monetary Fund and the World Bank. It controls interest rates, rediscounts bills, regulates the monetary system, fixes liquidity ratios, licenses the establishment of new banks, and has the power to replace the management of banks. It can also act to prevent the transfer of 25 percent or more of the shares in a bank.

The importance of monetary policy has been enhanced by the government's traditional inability to control its spending. High real interest rates, a consequence of tight monetary policy, fall mainly on the private sector. They increase the cost of debt to the government by pushing up the rate of interest that it has to pay on its bonds, which makes it more costly for the private sector to raise finance.

The 1954 act setting up the Bank of Israel listed its functions as the maintenance of price stability and high levels of employment and investment, along with the financial functions described above. These objectives came into conflict with one another in the late 1970s.

The bank is not fully in control of the channels through which monetary policy is conducted. This situation is mainly due to the government's traditional insistence on full, or near full, employment and the maintenance of high foreign exchange reserves. Until 1985, these constraints were compounded by very large budget deficits. Three other factors complicate the central bank's task. It is virtually unable to deal with the effects of inflows of foreign capital. The number of controls is so large that it is hard to maintain a consistent framework for monetary policy. Finally, the concentration of the banking system weakens its effectiveness.

Up to 1985, maintaining full employment and controlling the balance of payments were the main objectives of government policy. Until 1986 the Bank of Israel could, by law, extend unlimited credit to the Treasury. Despite very large budget deficits, monetary policy aimed to provide some parts of the private sector with credit. The external role of monetary policy was also important: Exporters received subsidized credits, and until 1985, exchange rate policy was mainly focused on dealing with balance-of-payments problems.

The bank's assets consist of net credit to the government, that to the private sector (mainly directed credit to exporters), and the monetary loan to the banking sector. On the liabilities side there are deposits of the banks, cash, and equity. Deposits include foreign currency and foreign currency–linked deposits.

The Bank of Israel imposes reserve requirements on the commercial banks: During the period 1977–1987 an average of 47 percent of local currency deposits had to be deposited in the central bank. Exemptions were granted for export financing, thus lowering the real reserve requirement. The banks seldom met these ratios and paid fines as a result, which indicates that the fines were not a deterrent, given the comparatively low rates of interest paid on the reserves at the central bank. Foreign currency–linked deposits, which increased dramatically between 1977 and 1985, were by their very nature protected against devaluation. They were also, until 1985, very liquid. As inflation and accompanying devaluations accelerated, the contribution of foreign currency–linked deposits to the growth of the broadly defined money supply increased.

Government direction of credit dates back to 1955, when special funds were set up to provide cheap credit for activities favored by the government. Some of these came from commercial bank resources. In return, those banks were permitted to have a higher reserve ratio than that prescribed by the Bank of Israel, and they were exempted from reserve requirements on funds made available to priority areas. The government supplemented these funds with others from its own deposits. These credits, which became known as directed credit, were lent at rates of interest lower than those available from the banks or on the so-called free or gray market of nonbank financial institutions, which meant that there was a range of interest rates for investment projects: As early as 1962 bank funds cost 8.4 percent, free market funds 17–19 percent, and directed credit 5.2 percent. These were nominal or actual interest rates on short-term credits during a period of relatively low inflation.[8] Since 1977 credit has been available in local and foreign currencies. During the period from January to October 1986, for example, when inflation was about 20 percent a year, short-term, free market credit cost 35 percent in real terms (about 55 percent in nominal terms), while directed credit for exports had a negative real interest rate of about 8 percent. Long-term funds on the free market cost 10 percent in real terms, and directed credit about 2.5 percent. The importance of directed credit has been considerable: In 1973 it accounted for 33.7 percent of total bank credit to the public; in 1979 it reached a peak of 48.2 percent; and in 1985 it came to 34.9 percent.[9] However, in 1986 only about 17 percent of credit was available through the free market.

Directed credit was provided to exporters in order to insulate them from the effects of domestic inflation. Most of it was short-term credit and was administered through the private banks. The Ministries of Industry and Finance were represented on the Bank of Israel committee that allocated most of these credits and decided on its costs. Between 1977 and 1987 about one-third of short-term bank credit was directed, leaving two-thirds nominally controlled by the Bank of Israel according to monetary policy criteria. This latter sector of credit received the full force of monetary control, and as a result interest rates tended to be high and volatile. The system of control and its consequences for monetary policy remain broadly unchanged. In the 1990 budget, $1.6 billion was allocated for directed credit.

The government also controls the quality and quantity of funds raised abroad, which in certain circumstances attract a 7.5 percent capital services levy. This control increased in the years up to 1985; in 1979 the government took 23 percent of domestic credit, and in 1983 it reached a peak of 59 percent.[10]

Despite many restrictions Israel is very exposed to foreign lending. Total short-term private debt as a share of GNP averaged 31 percent in the period 1980–1986. The authorities have favored longer term sources of finance on the grounds that they are more stable. There is what is called a general restriction on the right to borrow abroad, which is accompanied by significant exemptions. The market is, therefore, very segmented, with interest rates varying between different sectors, depending on the type of credit.

The Public's Financial Asset Portfolio

Table 6.1 shows how the composition of the public's short-term asset holdings has changed over the last decade. The period 1976–1980 was one of relative stability. As inflation reached very high levels in the period 1980–1983, the share of savings deposits declined: The share of foreign currency–linked bank deposits and shares rose correspondingly.

The share of foreign currency–linked deposits increased until the first half of 1985, when inflation was brought under control; the importance of nonbank shares started to decline with their collapse on the stock market in January 1983. The share of assets held in the form of bank shares fell much more sharply with their collapse on the stock exchange in the autumn of 1983. Unindexed assets have become more important since inflation was reduced in 1985, after a long period in which they were held at the minimum level needed for transaction purposes. From July 1985 until January 1987 the shekel's exchange rate was frozen and interest rates on shekel accounts were increased in order to encourage the holding of shekels rather than foreign currency. This move encouraged an increase in the share of nonindexed items such as shekel current and short-term deposit accounts.

Social Insurance Funds

Social insurance funds are the most important intermediaries in the capital market. Most household contractual savings go through them. Employees, employers, and the self-employed all contribute, and the balance, after payments of pensions and severance pay, is invested in government bonds and other financial assets.

The main component of the social insurance funds is pension funds. Provident funds (which provide cover for workers dismissed for various reasons) and study-leave funds (for professional workers) account for the rest. Employers' contributions to these funds are not taxable and the tax benefit is worth approximately $500 million a year. Most of this benefit accrues to those on higher earnings.[11] In 1985 social insurance funds and life insurance companies had $20.4 billion of assets, equal to 38 percent of the public's financial wealth. In 1988 the corresponding figures were $32.7 billion and 44 percent. The increase in their share of the total reflects the move into longer term assets that accompanied the reduction in inflation. Despite the growth of assets and the move to longer term investments, the corporate sector continues to suffer problems in attracting capital at a price that it can afford.

TABLE 6.1
Short-term Assets Held by the Nonfinancial Private Sector, 1977-1987
(end of year, percent)

	M1 [a]	Time deposits and CDs [b]	Foreign currency-linked deposits (of residents only)	Tradeable bonds	Total	Total as % of GNP
1977	24.7	6.5	22.1	46.7	100.0	55.0
1978	22.1	4.9	32.8	40.2	100.0	54.0
1979	14.3	3.3	46.3	36.1	100.0	57.1
1980	11.4	3.6	46.8	38.2	100.0	60.0
1981	10.2	5.3	52.9	31.6	100.0	51.1
1982	9.1	10.9	49.0	31.0	100.0	53.9
1983	6.6	8.9	60.8	23.7	100.0	66.2
1984	5.4	9.4	65.8	19.4	100.0	76.9
1985	7.3	25.2	47.4	20.1	100.0	50.3
1986	12.9	31.8	33.7	21.6	100.0	40.3
1987	14.3	36.0	25.6	24.1	100.0	41.2

a M1 is the narrowly defined supply of money: cash and demand deposits.
b CDs = certificates of deposit.

Sources: Annual Reports, Jerusalem: Bank of Israel, 1977 to 1987.

Some Implications for Corporate Finance

Companies in Israel cannot raise nonequity finance with ease. The government regulates their bond issues and has caused high interest rates in recent years because of its own funding program. Firms competed with the government for funds but were handicapped, given their size relative to the government. This situation has had implications for the structure of ownership and control: Large holding companies affiliated with the banks have an advantage over smaller private companies. As a result, many Israeli firms have underborrowed. The domination of the local market by the largest local banks and the extent of government controls have discouraged firms from borrowing abroad or using sources outside banking channels, despite an international trend toward using nonbank sources.[12] The availability of subsidized loans and grants also made use of the stock market less attractive. The disciplines that effective stock markets can exert were also absent. The stock market is dominated by the banks and by large institutional funds as well as by the government, which controls much of its activity.

During 1985, the government reduced subsidies, but the continuation of directed credit means that there is a form of credit rationing. Directed credit in foreign currency is charged at LIBOR (London Interbank Offered Rate) plus 2 percent, which is comparable with the cost of funds in Western Europe. The free market interest rate would be higher if there was no directed credit, and it is higher on nondirected funds; therefore, an implicit subsidy is involved.

Controls on the raising of private funds, together with preferential treatment given to approved enterprises under the Law for the Encouragement of Capital Investment, imply a major government role in the investment decisions of individual firms. Through the Industrial Development Bank the state has played an important part in financing investment: Between 1956 and 1968 development banks provided 60 percent of the funds used for investment in fixed assets. At that time only 25 percent of short-term bank credit granted to the manufacturing sector came from the uncontrolled funds of commercial banks. Seventy-five percent came from sources controlled by the government. Government funding on easy terms resulted in a very high level of investment in equipment and inventory. Funds were also reloaned to suppliers and customers helping to create a grey market in credit. It also enabled producers to extend credit, thus threatening the aims of monetary policy.

The other side of this situation is a debt to equity ratio that has been relatively low by international standards.[13] The failure of the equity market to develop in the period up to 1978 was due to the inability of the government to keep up with inflation. In 1966 the government started to offer borrowers insurance to protect them against linkage differentials. Recipients of index-linked credit could pay a fixed premium to the government in return for their linked liabilities. The government subsidized companies by fixing the premium at a low level relative to the expected rate of inflation.[14]

From 1985 to 1987 the redemption of bonds exceeded the issue of new ones. Only by virtue of linkage insurance was there a positive net flow of capital and this was achieved with government assistance. The issue of new shares rose fivefold in real terms between 1985 and 1987 but remained very small compared with the private sector's use of bank credit. The main change in these years was the massive growth of bank credit, which was due to reduced government control, made possible by its own reduced need for credit.

In the United States entrepreneurs are frequently forced to compete for development funds and, therefore, have to make their products saleable. In Israel there has, until recently, been little in the way of venture capital; entrepreneurs either obtain funds from the government or from one of the large conglomerates. In the latter case the entrepreneur may lose equity and therefore incentives. The financial system does not force entrepreneurs into contact with venture capitalists or marketing experts who would encourage them to increase their marketability. These are important institutional functions of the capital market that are missing in Israel.

The high cost of credit has led to the extensive development of a grey market; conglomerates act as bankers to their subsidiaries and associates rather than relying on the controlled credit system of the banks. Nonbank organizations also lend funds on this market.

The Banking System

Israel's banking system consists of twenty-five so-called ordinary banking corporations, which were subject to the liquidity regulations of the Bank of Israel, and thirty-five other banking and financial institutions. At the end of 1989 the ordinary banks employed 2.2 percent of the labor force, operated through just over 1,000 banking offices, and had assets of about $75 billion. The five main banking groups had total capital of nearly $4 billion and made profits of $150 million. Overseas subsidiaries and branches had assets of $18 billion, or $16 billion if intergroup assets are netted out. Sixty-six percent of these belonged to branches, subsidiaries, and representative offices in the United States. The scale of overseas activities is partly a reflection of the importance of Israel's external trade and the unwillingness of foreign banks to open offices in Israel. Israeli banks have been the beneficiaries of this lack of competition on the domestic market, and the largest of them have formed what is, in effect, a cartel, limiting competition.

The banking system has been increasingly dominated by a small number of large banks that, at least until recently, acted as investment analysts and advisers, underwriters, and stock and investment brokers. The banks issue most of the share capital and debentures of quoted companies, and they manage the sale of government bonds and short-term assets. They carry out all foreign exchange transactions and, through their investment and insurance companies, administer savings schemes. All this is in addition to their regular functions as commercial banks. The three largest banks, Leumi Le Israel (Leumi), HaPoalim, and Discount, held 56 percent of the banking system's assets in 1955 and 82 percent in 1987.

At the end of 1989 Bank Leumi had assets of $31 billion. It had 14,000 employees in 412 branches and offices, seventy of which were abroad. In Israel, it owns 85.5 percent of the Union Bank, as well as two other banks. It has four overseas subsidiaries and six finance companies and owns 89.9 percent of Africa-Israel, one of the largest property development companies in the country. In addition it has insurance and trust companies, mutual and provident funds, and major shareholdings in a credit card corporation. Most of its shares are owned by a holding company that in turn is owned by the Jewish Agency, a semiautonomous state body.

Bank Leumi's origins go back to the Jewish Colonial Trust, set up in 1899 at the initiative of Theodore Herzl, founder of the modern Zionist movement. The aim was to use the company to finance the development of the Jewish economy in Palestine. In 1903 the Anglo-Palestine Company was founded by the trust and was indirectly controlled by the World Zionist Organization. In 1951 the Anglo-Palestine Company was renamed Bank Leumi, and with the independence of the state in 1948, it was given the right to issue currency. This right lasted until 1954 when the Bank of Israel was created as the central bank.

Bank HaPoalim, controlled by the Histadrut's Hevrat Ovdim, has assets totalling $30 billion. In 1985 it had 341 branches in Israel and thirty-two branches and subsidiaries in fourteen countries abroad. It owns seven other banks in Israel and four abroad, as well as two mortgage banks, three investment and financial companies, and four financial advisory companies.

The Israel Discount Bank was founded in 1935 and is the largest privately owned bank and third largest bank in the country. It has assets worth about $13 billion. Its parent company, IDB Bankholding Corporation, Ltd., is one of the largest investment groups in Israel, with shares in numerous other companies including sixteen involved in banking.

The Bank Share Collapse of 1983 and Its Aftermath

With the acceleration of inflation in the late 1970s, the demand for banking services increased. The banks were also engaged in rapid expansion programs at the time. In order to finance this growth they required increased capital that could not be raised with ease in a capital market dominated by the government.

Government controls on interest rates and the tax system squeezed the profits of an already inefficient sector to virtually nothing by the end of 1983. The banks, therefore, turned to the share market to raise new capital; the only way in which they could compete with the government was to effectively convert their shares into something like index-linked bonds. The prices of their shares were "regulated" by the banks to ensure that they rose at least as fast as inflation. In this way they attracted new buyers and discouraged sellers.

In order to increase the value of their shares in the capital market, given the dominant role of the government, the banks pushed up the prices of their own shares on the Tel Aviv Stock Exchange (TASE). According to the official commission of enquiry, regulation of the banks' shares began as early as 1972. It became significant in distorting markets from the period 1978–1979. Until 1983, in order to offer a yield of up to 30 percent or more in real terms, the banks regulated the price of their own shares by encouraging their customers to buy their shares and by buying them themselves. With these high rates of return, the banks were able to compete with the different forms of government bonds available to the public and thus raise capital. Imported finance was also used by the banks to buy their own shares, with subsidiaries abroad playing a key role. All of this activity took place against a background of profitability that failed to increase in line with the yield on their shares,[15] which would normally result in a downward trend in the price of the shares or would at least dampen any increase. Conditions were far from normal, however. According to the official commission of enquiry, the value of bank shares increased from $470 million in 1975 to $4.0 billion in 1981 and $6.8 billion in September 1983. This value included new shares issued during the period.[16] In order to compete with the government for funds, the banks offered incredibly high rates of return, thereby succeeding in attracting massive investment, especially as it was encouraged by the most influential source of investment advice in the country: the banks themselves. According to a member of the commission of enquiry, such an environment made economic efficiency, investors' interests, and even enforcement of the law expendable, and the collapse of the market became inevitable. In the summer of 1983, about 500,000 individuals owned approximately $4 billion of bank shares, companies and other bodies owned about $2 billion, and the banks themselves held $1.2 billion.[17] At the end of September 1983 some selling began as a result of expectations of a long-overdue devaluation. In early October the public started to sell large quantities of shares in order to buy foreign currency–linked deposits. Initial sales were made at very high prices, up to 325 percent of the capital and reserve value of the shares. Very quickly the bottom fell out of the market as the banks became unable to support the price of their shares, due to the volume of sales. They tried to import funds in order to buy back their shares, but this attempt failed to stem the tide.

The government was forced to step in: The TASE was closed for a week. An agreement was reached whereby the shares of the banks were considered as dollar-denominated government bonds. The face value was set at 85 percent of the precrash market price, far higher than the rate that would have evolved had the market for the shares been allowed to take its course without government intervention. The arrangement meant that the government would pay 3 percent interest on the bonds, which were linked to the dollar and could be redeemed in five years. The government in effect issued bonds to replace the shares. In 1989, an official report indicated that the total cost of the bank share rescue package would come to $8.1 billion, including the costs of the final redemption in 1991.[18] In order to discourage the public from selling their shares, which would have resulted in a de facto nationalization of the banks, the banks, beginning in 1983, made strenuous efforts to increase their profitability. In so doing they hoped to make their shares attractive for the public to hold on to. Their success in this is examined below.

The government's aim in guaranteeing the bank shares was to ensure that the banks remained independent. This condition was deemed essential because of their centrality in the economy, their contribution to Israel's foreign trade, and their importance in raising funds abroad.[19] The reality of their independence is questionable, however, given that the Jewish Agency, a quasi-governmental body, owns many of the shares in the largest bank, Bank Leumi. The examiner of banks at the Bank of Israel considered the perception of the banks as independent to be vital. Explicit government control and ownership had to be avoided. A scandal, in January 1987, over enormous payments made to the dismissed managing director of Bank Leumi, despite the blame placed on him by the official commission of enquiry into the bank share collapse, reopened the issue of control.

In 1986 the official commission of inquiry into the regulation of the bank shares concluded its work and issued a report fiercely critical of the banks, their directors, and the government. It concluded that the regulation of the bank shares was illegal, undermined the banks' stability, and damaged the economy. The commission also concluded that the banks had manipulated the prices of shares in associated companies; the heads of the four largest banks were ordered to be removed from their positions and the government was told to remove the governor of the Bank of Israel from office. It recommended that the banks be barred from direct and indirect share trading on their behalf, that they be prevented from managing trust funds, either directly or indirectly, and that investment managers be independent of the banks and come under the supervision of the Securities Authority. The banks would be allowed to act as trustees for pension funds but would not be allowed to encourage consultants to urge the purchase of shares favored by the banks.

Another official committee recommended that the banks be barred from advising on securities purchases and that a license be required for bank employees giving investment advice. In general terms the official commission recommended less government intervention in the capital market but more regulation through such bodies as the Securities Authority.

In January 1983 there had been a collapse of nonbank shares. The years 1980 to 1983 were ones of an extraordinary, speculative bubble: Many shares rose by 400 percent in dollar terms, despite hyperinflation and declining profitability. The Law for Taxation under Conditions of Inflation contributed to the collapse of nonbank share prices by imposing a tax on the increase in the value of shares whether or not they were sold. By the end of 1983 many shares were back to their 1980 level.

After 1983: The Banks and the Problem of the Bank Shares

Until 1983 the government held down interest rates, and bank charges did not rise with inflation. Following the collapse of their share prices, the banks started to lay off staff in order to reduce costs. They also reduced the number of bank branches inside Israel from 1,125 in 1983 to 1,066 in 1985.[20] In March 1987 the Bank of Israel called for the closure of another fifty branches. Monetary policy also changed: Interest rates rose and in 1985 bank charges were temporarily decontrolled.

Between 1983 and 1986 the five largest banks—Leumi, HaPoalim, Discount, Mizrachi, and the First International—had total profits of only $68 million. In 1986, according to the examiner of banks at the Bank of Israel, the major banks were in a very weak position. Their total assets were 16 percent lower than in 1984, there was a recession in the demand for their services, and 63 percent of their profits were derived from unlinked shekel deposits, which accounted for only 5 percent of their balance sheets.[21] They also had a large number of bad debts on their books, in part a result of general economic conditions. Posttax profits of the five major banks in 1987 rose to $300 million, after allowing $500 million for bad debts. The examiner pointed out that these relatively high profits were achieved on a very narrow section of the banks' business and resulted from the wide gap in interest rates on loans and deposits in unlinked shekels. The financial results for the five main banking corporations in 1989 and 1990 show that this reliance for profit on a narrow section of business continued to be a problem.

The government is now in the process of selling the shares it owns in the banks. It hopes through sales to recover part of the $8 billion spent from 1983.

Conclusion

The financial sector has been dominated by the government's need to recycle its huge internal debt and pay interest on it. Although the budget deficits, which caused the growth in debt, have declined, they continue and need financing. Financing the deficit can no longer be done by printing money because of legal restrictions.

The capital markets have had to cope with index-linked government debt on such a scale that private sector borrowers have had very limited access. The Bank of Israel is also handicapped in its operation of monetary policy, both by the need to fund government debt and by a complex system of legal controls that segments financial markets and limits competition. The main commercial banks collapsed in the misguided attempt to compete with the government for funds in 1983, and as a result they were effectively nationalized.

Relatively high inflation and the size of the internal debt make an opening of the financial sector to foreign competition problematic. This opening is very gradually being achieved and is a necessary condition for economic growth.

Notes

1. *Annual Report 1990* (Jerusalem: Bank of Israel, 1990). In Hebrew.
2. Bank of Israel data.
3. E. Kleiman, *The Indexation of the Public Sector Debt in Israel* (Jerusalem: Maurice Falk Institute for Economic Research in Israel, May 1985).
4. M. Sarnat, "Monetary Risk, Stagflation and the Uneasy Case for Indexation," in M. Sarnat, ed., *Inflation and Capital Markets* (Cambridge, Mass.: Ballinger, 1978).
5. *Main Points of the Budget, 1988* (Jerusalem: Ministry of Finance, 1988). In Hebrew.
6. *Ha'aretz* (Tel Aviv), 1 November 1989. In Hebrew.
7. *Annual Report 1989* (Jerusalem: Bank of Israel, 1990).

8. *Annual Reports 1973, 1979, 1985* (Jerusalem: Bank of Israel 1974, 1980, 1986).

9. *International Financial Statistics 1983 Yearbook* (Washington, D.C.: International Monetary Fund, 1984).

10. Kleiman, *The Indexation of the Public Sector Debt in Israel.*

11. *Main Points of the Budget, 1986* (Jerusalem: Ministry of Finance, 1986). In Hebrew.

12. *Economist* (London), 7 June 1986.

13. M. Tamari, *Some International Comparisons of Industrial Financing* (Stonehouse, Gloucester, England: Technicopy, Ltd., 1977).

14. Sarnat, "Monetary Risk, Stagflation and the Uneasy Case for Indexation."

15. *Annual Survey 1983, 1984, 1985* (Jerusalem: Examiner of Banks, Bank of Israel). In Hebrew.

16. *Report of the Commission of Enquiry into the Regulation of the Bank Shares,* Appendix Aleph, Table 14, p. Nun 19.

17. *Economist,* 15 October 1983.

18. *Ha'aretz,* 6 November 1989.

19. *Annual Survey 1986* (Jerusalem: Examiner of Banks, 1986).

20. *Asakim* supplement to *Ma'ariv* (Tel Aviv), 17 June 1986, in Hebrew, and *Industrial Israel* (Tel Aviv), October 1985.

21. *Annual Survey 1986.*

7

Labor

The Labor movement, which dominated the political and economic development of Israel from 1948 to 1977, consisted of the Histadrut, the General Federation of Labor with its affiliated bodies, and the Labor party. The Histadrut, both as a trade union organization and as one of the largest employers in the country, plays a central role in the economy and in the provision of social services; it has considerable political influence.

This chapter is concerned with much more than labor as a factor of production in the narrow economic sense. It examines the institutions of the Labor movement and their roles, as well as basic economic factors, such as the supply of labor, wages, and their effects on the distribution of income.

The dominant version of Zionism, at least until 1977, was the socialist one that evolved out of European, left-wing ideologies at the end of the nineteenth and early twentieth centuries. Collective action was regarded, at least until the early 1960s, as the most effective way to realize national interests. The dominant ideology viewed profits as parasitic and services as unproductive. Under conditions of war and mass immigration, such as those existing in 1948, a form of socialism seemed natural to those who led the country.[1]

In 1948 Israel was, in terms of the distribution of income and its social ethos, an egalitarian society. The Labor party and its left-wing allies dominated the life of the state, despite an early policy introduced by the first prime minister and Labor leader, David Ben Gurion, to build up state rather than party institutions. This policy meant that much of what was done by sectoral or political groups before independence (such as providing educational and employment services) was to be carried out by the government. The most significant changes were the welding of military groups into the Israel Defense Forces, the introduction of state education systems, and the government's increased responsibility for social welfare and employment.

As a result Israel in the 1940s and 1950s had a pioneering atmosphere. The enormous cost of the War of Independence, in which 1 percent of the Jewish population was killed, and the effects of the Holocaust in Europe were the background to a major effort of national renewal. There was little to buy and most of the population had a low standard of living, but there was a sense of mission. During the 1960s, as living standards rose, the sense of mission declined; it has now virtually disappeared. Income inequality and relative poverty are considerable, and the distribution of wealth is very unequal. (There are no official statistics on the distribution of wealth, but even the most casual observations in a small society make this conclusion obvious.)

The Ideology of the Labor Movement

Labor Zionists came to Palestine in order to create a new type of Jewish society and a new type of Jew. They wanted to return to manual labor, particularly on the land, and to change the Jewish psyche and society by building a socialist economy in which people would be self-reliant and value work. They wanted Jews to do all kinds of jobs and have access to all sectors of the economy, which had not occurred in the diaspora. In this sense their mission was revolutionary. Services were considered parasitic and intellectuals were viewed ambiguously by labor leaders.

This ideology gave rise to many conflicts in the preindependence period. The Socialist Zionists often sought fraternal relations with Arab workers and peasants and wanted to include Arabs in the Histadrut but opposed the employment of the latter by Jewish capitalists at lower wages than Jews would take. More recently there have been ideological conflicts over whether Arabs and others should be employed in kibbutzim as outside workers.

Events since 1948 have also weakened the ideology of the Labor movement. The arrival, after 1948, of many unskilled Jews from North Africa and the Middle East led to their employment in low-status positions. They were often sent to development areas, where basic industries were set up to employ them. These industries were not established on a completely economic basis, and the immigrant workers were employed at low wages. With the education of the younger generation, productivity and real wages rose, but this earlier generation of Jews failed to take leading positions in the Labor-run economy and Histadrut.

Although Arabs were encouraged to join the Histadrut beginning in the 1920s, attempts to prevent their employment in the Jewish economy continued up to the early 1950s. The aim was to maintain employment and wages for the mass of often unskilled Jewish immigrants. Gradually this effort broke down, and Arabs started to work in Jewish agriculture and in particular in construction.

These patterns were reinforced after 1967, when Israel gained control of the West Bank and Gaza, with a population of 1 million. Arabs from the West Bank and Gaza tended to supplant Jews of Middle Eastern and North African origin in low-status occupations such as construction work. The latter moved up the ladder in terms of their work status, gaining jobs in the service and public sectors.

Since the 1960s there has been a reversal of the Jewish work ethic as enunciated by the Socialist Zionists. The service sector has grown, and Arabs are employed in the manual jobs that Jews do not want. The idea that manual labor would contribute to the redemption of the Jewish people also came into conflict with the desire, and the need, for higher education. In a country lacking raw materials and fuel deposits, it was realized that the labor force was virtually the only economic resource. Increasing its skill level would, therefore, make an important contribution to economic development. Investment in education and training increased, which reduced the prestige of agriculture, construction, and other forms of manual labor. Strong central government, with its large bureaucracy, became a growing source of employment in the service sector; inflation led to the growth of financial services, especially banking. These factors reinforced the movement away from manual and industrial employment.

The Histadrut

The Histadrut, or General Federation of Labor, was founded in 1920 as a comprehensive organization for Jewish workers in the Yishuv. Its range of activities covered trade union matters, the development of new rural settlements, agriculture, industry, banking, insurance, housing, construction, transportation, social services, and cultural activities. The original and basic aim was to create employment for Jewish workers in Palestine. By generating full employment, high living standards, and job security, the organization would help Jewish workers achieve personal dignity.

In accordance with its philosophy of acting comprehensively and in lieu of the government, in 1921 the Histadrut set up Bank HaPoalim (the Workers' Bank). Two years later Hevrat Ovdim (the Workers' Company or Cooperative Federation) was created from the Bureau of Public and Construction Workers. By 1925, Hevrat Ovdim was acting as the holding company for all the communities' cooperatives. Cooperatives were organized for dairy production and for bus transportation. By 1930 Hamashbir, the retail cooperative; Hasneh, the insurance company; and others were incorporated into Hevrat Ovdim.

Histadrut enterprises expanded their investments by reinvesting their profits. In 1927, when the Solel Boneh Construction Company went bankrupt, Histadrut leaders realized the importance of maintaining independent capital resources. Capital accumulation designed to meet the needs of its enterprises replaced job creation as the Histadrut's primary objective.[2] This practice limited the vulnerability and exposure of its companies and economic organizations to changes in the economy and government policy.

With the independence of Israel, the Histadrut transferred some of its functions to the national government. These included education, some labor exchanges that had been under its control, social welfare services, housing, and assistance for new immigrants. Significantly, as will be seen in Chapter 8, it retained control over Kupat Holim Clalit, the health fund.

Independence brought large government development budgets that financed much of the country's investment. Histadrut enterprises no longer needed to rely on their profits to maintain investment levels. They concentrated on the development of new plants in outlying regions of the country, in accordance with the government's population dispersal policy. Insofar as profitability was neglected, so Histradrut enterprises such as Koor, Solel Boneh, Kupat Holim Clalit, and the Egged Bus Cooperative were badly placed to deal with the radical changes in economic policy that came in the late 1970s and 1980s.

In recent years many Histadrut enterprises such as Koor and Tadiran have ceased to make profits. Solel Boneh suffered its second financial collapse and has been merged with another Histadrut company in the construction sector. The losses in firms belonging to the industrial holding company, Koor, totalled $303 million in 1989, an enormous sum in Israeli terms. Profits fell from the modest level of $43 million in 1982 continuously until 1986. In the period 1987–1989 the group accumulated losses of $854 million.[3] The political leadership of the Histadrut wanted both profits and higher wages, something that was only possible with higher productivity increases than those achieved. It also insisted that all workers be paid cost-of-living and other wage and salary increases regardless of the profitability of their company, which brought about the resignation of Koor's managing director. As losses accumulated, the Histadrut's ability to finance them declined. The government, for financial and political reasons, was unwilling to bail out bankrupt operations to the same extent as it had in the past, and the trade union organization was unwilling to lay off workers.

The problems facing Koor are partly the result of general trends in the economy affecting other industrial sectors. Owners of companies in all sectors did not fully understand that the government had, at least in part, ended its role as the financier of development. They suffered from huge increases in interest rates in 1985 and failed to realize that devaluations would not necessarily protect exports against rising costs at home. The problem was compounded in the Histadrut sector by the policy of not making workers redundant and the fact that wage increases were, to a large extent, imposed from above. In the summer of 1988 reforms were announced reducing the power of the trade union department to force wage increases on Histadrut enterprises. Firms were to be sold or closed if they did not make profits. If fully implemented, this reform will amount to an ideological shift of major significance: The Histadrut will be bowing to market forces that it tried, so far unsuccessfully, to resist. It will also be returning to the policy that it adopted in the prestate period, when emphasis was placed on maintaining financial independence rather than maximizing employment. A number of companies have been sold, but worker resistance to the closing of others has brought delays in the implementation of the program.

Protection of Histadrut enterprises impinges on national wage negotiations. In order to obtain economic help for Kupat Holim and its pension funds, the Histadrut has made concessions on other matters in its negotiations with the government and private sector employers. The involvement of health and pension fund considerations has enormously complicated negotiations, which very often have a hidden as well as a stated agenda.

The problems faced in the cooperative sector have resulted in the sale of some firms to the private sector, but there have been virtually no experiments in terms of worker participation in management or direct ownership. This lack of innovation is perhaps surprising given the existence of kibbutz industries within the same sector.

The Structure of the Histadrut

The leadership of the Histadrut is elected by its members, and the Labor party has had an absolute majority since its foundation. There are about 1.6 million members and members' spouses in the Histadrut, including 165,000 Arabs and Druze. Elections to the Histadrut convention take place every four years, lists of candidates being submitted by the political parties. The convention elects members to the council, which in turn elects the executive committee. The trade union department is also made up of political representatives in proportion to their representation in the convention. Workers' committees are elected on a nonpolitical basis at the place of employment. The Histadrut is a federation of trade unions with the standard function of representing workers in negotiations with employers on wages, benefits, and conditions. There are seventy-two local labor councils that handle matters at the community level and act as a link with the leadership. The Histadrut undertakes social, cultural, and educational activities; runs sports, youth and student organizations; and has a women's branch and an institute for the training of labor leaders from developing countries. Bus cooperatives, the country's main dairy cooperative, and a large chain of supermarkets are affiliated with the Histadrut.

The Histadrut has always been controlled by the Labor party, which has won a majority in all the elections to the convention. As a result it has often been described as a "state within a state."

Communal and Collective Settlements

The kibbutz, a phenomenon unique to Israel, is built on the basis of complete equality of all of its members and on the communal ownership and provision of all services. Members do not receive an income; they get all the services they require without charge and are given a small monetary allowance to spend outside the kibbutz. Most significant, from an economic point of view, is the fact that allowances are not, in any way, related to the individual's work effort. Only in extreme cases will a member be asked to leave the kibbutz if his efforts are considered unsatisfactory.

The lack of connection between effort and income (taken in the form of services and allowances) should, according to much conventional economic thinking, result in inefficiency and even financial collapse. The kibbutzim have, however, achieved high living standards and impressive agricultural and industrial growth. They have also resisted the trend toward urbanization; their population has not fallen as has that of other rural settlements. They have been successful innovators in agriculture and have undertaken a major industrialization in response to market forces. The marginal productivity of labor has been higher in kibbutz industry and agriculture than elsewhere in the economy, and, at least until recently, they were efficient in the use of capital.[4] In the last five years the kibbutzim have faced severe financial difficulties because of problems in agriculture (discussed in Chapter 4) and because of bad industrial and financial investments that were, in part, started before the large increases in interest rates in 1985. They have had to reduce living standards and cut back on investments while negotiating for government assistance in coping with their debts to the commercial banks.

In 1947, there were 176 kibbutzim and about 44,000 people were living on them.[5] At the end of 1988, there were 270 kibbutzim with 126,000 inhabitants. In 1988, 256 kibbutzim were affiliated with Hevrat Ovdim.

Another, much smaller, type of settlement associated with the Labor movement is the Moshav Shitufi, or collective village. In these groups, individual households provide most of their own services. Income is shared and work organized communally. At the end of 1988 there were forty-seven Moshav Shitufi, with 11,000 inhabitants.

Moshavim are villages that were originally set up on the basis of private farming, with each individual or family receiving only as much land as it could farm. Residents share some services and are responsible for each others' debts. Marketing and procurement are organized by the Moshav movement as a whole. Moshavim have suffered even more than the kibbutzim from bad investments and the general problems facing agriculture. In an atmosphere of increased economic accountability, the economic viability of many moshavim is now in question. At the end of 1988 there were 409 moshavim, with 147,000 inhabitants.

Population

The raison d'être of the state of Israel is to bring Jews back to their homeland; the Law of Return contains a clause giving all Jews the right to live in Israel and become citizens. Encouragement of immigration, be it providing information to students on U.S. campuses, flying Ethiopian Jews to Israel in secret, or campaigning for the right of Soviet Jews to emigrate, is, therefore, part of official ideology. Assistance in housing, absorption, language teaching, and employment is given to all immigrants.

As early as 1937, a British royal commission noted how important the role of immigrants was in increasing the capital stock in Mandatory Palestine.[6] In the period after 1948 mass immigration brought a less-skilled population to Israel with little financial capital. The immigration of hundreds of thousands of North African and Middle Eastern Jews in the early 1950s initially lowered the average educational and skill level of the population. Later, their absorption led to a major increase in productivity levels that contributed to rapid economic growth in the late 1950s and 1960s.

Child allowances, provision of mother and baby clinics, and other transfers have been used to encourage natural population growth. This goal was considered vital, given the loss of one-third of the world Jewish population in the Holocaust between 1933 and 1945 and the continuous state of war in which Israel found itself.

The decline in the rate of population growth has contributed to lower economic growth in recent years. Increased emigration and a lower level of immigration from the West have also been responses to economic and political changes in Israel.[7] The number arriving in Israel on immigrant visas fell continuously from 1979 to 1989. In the period 1980–1988 the average was 6,000 per annum. (In addition, over 6,000 arrived on other visas and changed their status to that of immigrant in 1988.) Approximately 73 percent came from Europe (including the USSR) and North and South

America, the rest from Africa and Asia. The slowdown after 1979 largely reflected the decline in the number of Soviet Jews allowed to emigrate. In the same period there was an increase in the number arriving from Africa, mainly the result of the rescue of Ethiopian Jews organized by Israel and the United States.

In the last few months of 1989 an upsurge in immigration from the Soviet Union began. Total immigration in 1989 reached 24,000, and in 1990, 199,500, mostly from the USSR. Approximately 170,000 arrived in 1991. This surge has had significant effects on the economy, increasing demand, especially for housing, and adding many skilled workers to the labor force. It also increased the economic growth rate. The immigration from the USSR contains a high percentage of academics and doctors. Increased allocations were made for immigrant services in the 1990 and 1991 budgets, the implications of which are examined in the next chapter. The first of these immigrants started looking for work at the end of 1990. This immigration has caused an increase in the size of the labor force, both employed and unemployed.

Emigration is a sensitive issue in Israel, in view of the Zionist ideology of bringing Jews to the country. It has detrimental effects on national morale and on the supply of skilled labor. The cumulative balance from May 15, 1948, to the end of 1988 of residents who remained abroad for four years or longer came to 293,000. If an emigrant is defined as someone who was out of the country for one year or more, the total was 376,500, excluding an estimated 40,000 to 50,000 who had died. Approximately 50 percent of the emigrants left Israel since 1973.[8]

The Development of the Labor Force

Three main groups can be identified on an ethnic basis: Jews with an Oriental heritage, those with a Western one, and the Arabs of Israel. The Israeli-born Jewish population can be subdivided along the lines of the first two groups. Table 7.1 shows that the percentage of the population born in Africa and Asia with thirteen or more years of schooling rose from 3 percent in 1962 to 13.6 percent in 1989. The share of that group with less than eight years of education fell by nearly 30 percent. The degree of change among those born in Europe, America, and Israel was equally dramatic.

Among the non-Jewish population there has been an increase in educational levels, but it has been much less than that of other sections of the community.[9] During the 1980s the increase in educational levels among the non-Jewish group was minimal. The increase in educational levels for the majority did not, until recently, result in an oversupply of educated workers because demand for skills increased along with supply. The

TABLE 7.1
Persons over Age 14 by Years of Schooling and Continent of Birth, 1961-1989
(Both sexes, percent)

	Years of Schooling	AA	EA	Israel	ISAA	ISEA	Jews	Non-Jews
1961	0-8	77.8	48.7	30.4	60.9	15.7	55.5	90.9
	9-12	19.2	38.5	54.2	34.5	64.6	34.6	7.6
	13+	3.0	12.7	15.3	4.5	19.6	9.8	1.5
1972	0-8	67.5	41.4	21.4	35.7	9.3	44.1	81.8
	9-12	27.5	39.3	60.1	59.3	61.7	41.7	15.5
	13+	5.0	19.3	18.5	5.0	29.0	14.2	2.7
1985	0-8	50.7	29.6	9.6	13.9	4.0	25.4	53.1
	9-12	38.1	39.3	63.3	72.2	50.2	50.2	38.5
	13+	11.2	31.1	27.1	13.7	45.8	24.4	8.4
1989	0-8	47.9	27.1	6.5	9.3	3.3	21.3	52.1
	9-12	38.5	38.5	63.4	73.1	48.0	51.1	39.5
	13+	13.6	34.5	29.1	17.6	48.7	27.6	8.4

AA = born in Asia or Africa.
EA = born in Europe or Americas.
ISAA = born in Israel with Asian- or African- born father.
ISEA = born in Israel with European- or American- born father.

Sources: 1961-1972: Y. Ben Porath in Y. Ben Porath ed The Israeli Economy: Maturing Through Crises p. 159, Cambridge Mass: Harvard University Press, 1986; 1985: Statistical Abstract of Israel, 1986, Jerusalem: Central Bureau of Statistics, 1986.1989: Statistical Abstract of Israel, 1990, Jerusalem: Central Bureau of Statistics 1990.

relative pay of the educated sections of the labor force did not therefore fall. High-technology industries, financial services, and the public sector were the main sources of demand.[10] The arrival of large numbers of immigrants from the Soviet Union is further increasing the skill level of the population: A higher percentage of these newcomers have university or higher education than veteran Israelis.

The cuts in the government's budget in recent years have meant that it is no longer easily possible to substantially increase public services and employment facilities in order to deal with social divisions. Despite gaps in educational and occupational status between Jews of different communities, key variables in their home environments are converging. Family size, increased intermarriage, and residential and educational integration are all making for faster convergence among those born in Israel. This trend is taking place against a background of increased inequality in the distribution of income and wealth. The social convergence has not occurred between Arabs and Jews in Israel mainly because of political tension and cultural and social differences and because government policy has not been directed toward overcoming such differences.[11]

The share of professionals, scientists, and academics in the labor force has more than doubled since 1960; that of managers, administrators, and clerks grew by 39 percent, while more sophisticated methods and technology permitted a sharp reduction in the number of farmers and of blue-collar workers. One indication of the structural change is the deployment of engineers. In 1972 there were 9,825 engineers and 1,970 systems analysts and programmers in Israel. Only 1.2 percent of employees in manufacturing were engineers. By 1983 the number of engineers had more than doubled to 23,660; there were 7,685 systems analysts and programmers, and engineers accounted for 3.0 percent of employees in industry. By 1985 the share had increased to 3.4 percent. Of these engineers, 57 percent were employed in transportation and the electric and electronic branches. The same was true for technicians.

Current Labor Issues

Labor Force Participation

Israel's labor force participation rate is low compared to other developed economies. Table 7.2 shows that in 1990, 32 percent of the national population was employed (equal to 52 percent of the working age population) compared to about 48 percent in the United Kingdom and the United States. Israel's smaller share is due to the size of the armed services, the larger proportion of students, and the relatively low participation ratio of women in the work force. Women's participation rate was 38 percent in

TABLE 7.2
The Labor Force, 1980, 1985, and 1990
(Annual average, thousands)

	1980	1985	1990
Population, total	3922	4233	4659
Population aged 15+	2661	2853	3201
Civilian labor force	1318	1446	1650
Workers from administered territories	77	92	108
Employed [a]	1254	1349	1492
Unemployed [a]	34	97	158
Civilian labor force as percent of population	49.6	50.7	51.5
Unemployed as percent of labor force	5.0	6.7	9.6

[a] Excludes workers from Administered Territories.

Sources: 1980-1985: Statistical Abstract of Israel, Jerusalem: Central Bureau of Statistics, 1981 and 1986; 1985 Annual Report, Jerusalem, Bank of Israel, 1986. 1990: Monthly Bulletin of Statistics, March 1991, Jerusalem: Central Bureau of Statistics; 1988 Annual Report, Jerusalem: Bank of Israel, 1989; 1989 Annual Report, Jerusalem: Bank of Israel, 1990.

1984 compared to 42 percent in the United Kingdom and 44 percent in the United States. The female participation rate rose by nearly 10 percent in the period 1955–1972, while the male rate fell. The length of compulsory military service was lengthened during that period for men, thus reducing the supply available for civilian employment.

The growth of public services has taken an increasing share of civilian employment: from 23 percent in 1972 to 29 percent in 1980 and 1990 (see Table 7.3). Much of the growth in employment in Israel went into non-internationally traded sectors. During the period 1975–1984, only one out of seven additional employees was taken on by industry. Six went to services, of which three went to the public sector. The number of persons employed in the service sector per 100 residents increased from 18.9 in 1974 to 21.1 in mid-1985. In public and community services alone, the growth was from 8.3 in 1974 to 9.4 in mid-1985. Growth resumed in 1988 and 1989.

One reason for the increase in services was a rise in national expenditure on education and health. Another was that the public sector has become an employer of last resort. The third was increased social welfare and defense costs. An increasing share of services in the economy has

TABLE 7.3
Employment by Sector, 1980, 1985, and 1990
(thousands) [a]

	1980	1985	1990
Agriculture, forestry and fishing	79.2	72.1	61.7
Manufacturing and mining	294.3	309.3	322.2
Electricity and water	12.8	11.8	16.6
Construction	79.2	72.2	75.9
Commerce, restaurants and hotels	145.2	167.7	216.4
Transport, storage and communications	86.0	86.3	92.5
Finance and business services	102.0	131.2	148.4
Public and community services	367.9	403.0	439.2
Personal and other services	76.8	88.5	109.4
Unknown	11.0	7.2	9.6
Total	1,254.4	1,349.3	1,491.9

[a] Excludes workers from Administered Territories.

Sources: Statistical Abstract of Israel 1983, Jerusalem: Central Bureau of Statistics, and Monthly Bulletin of Statistics, Jerusalem: Central Bureau of Statistics, March 1991.

been a common phenomenon in the West, but the share of services in Israel is markedly higher than in other countries with a similar level of per capita national income.

In analyzing these figures, it is important to note that the large and growing public sector has been protected during economic crises. It proved extremely difficult to reduce public services and make civil servants redundant even during deep recessions such as those of 1966–1967 or 1988–1990. As a result, the burden of economic adjustment has fallen on the business sector.

The absorption of labor by the public sector, preventing, until recently, the emergence of unemployment, has been a fundamental mechanism at work in the labor market. It has contributed to inflation and thus worsened the economy's competitiveness. It also prevented downward pressure being exerted on real wages in the business sector and in the economy as a whole.[12] Only with the emergence of high levels of unemployment during 1989 did wages cease to exert significant inflationary pressures.

Unemployment

Comparatively low unemployment has, until recently, spared Israel some of the social problems faced in Europe and the United States. Unemployment has, however, affected levels of relative poverty and income inequality. Israel has had a very strong preference for full employment resulting from the desire to encourage immigration and prevent emigration and because of fears of the social consequences of unemployment.

As a result, until recently the rate of unemployment has been much lower in Israel than in many Western countries. Between 1982 and 1985 it averaged 5.5 percent of the labor force compared to 8.4 percent in the United States, 12.6 percent in the United Kingdom, 7.1 percent in West Germany, and 2.6 percent in Japan.[13] After 1973, the expansion of the army and the continued growth of civilian public services were the bases for lower unemployment. During 1988 and 1989 industry and services began to shed labor as part of a belated adjustment to the 1985 policy changes and in response to the recession that affected the economy. Since 1989 this situation has changed: Unemployment has risen to levels exceeding those in many European countries. In the second quarter of 1991 the seasonally adjusted unemployment rate was 10.8 percent, higher than the rate in the United States, the United Kingdom, or Germany.

The arrival of large numbers of immigrants at a time of high unemployment is causing considerable anxiety. The arguments about the best policy to be adopted follow the traditional lines of economic debate: Should a more urgent attempt be made to decentralize and liberalize the economy, or is the private sector too weak to provide the extra jobs needed? There is a consensus among economists about the need for less government intervention and so the debate now centers on the timing of reforms. An analysis of the changes needed is made in Chapter 9.

The Dual Economy

Industrial employment is characterized by a significant dualism. One important group is the engineering-scientific-managerial elite that is employed in high-technology industries. It is part of what Marcuse called the "World Village": characterized by people who read English and are closely in touch with economic, social, and cultural trends in the West, especially in the United States. Many could get work abroad, and large numbers have, particularly in the United States. This ability of elite workers to secure employment abroad affects the reward system in Israel: Not only has full employment been considered essential in order to prevent emigration but some members of this elite are paid salaries at U.S. levels in order to keep them in the country. Growing pressure to reduce the burden of income tax is also a result of the need to reward this group. At the opposite pole are the low-paid factory workers in such industries as textiles and food. The competitive advantage of these industries lies in low-cost production based on the availability of cheap labor. An increase in the number of those in employment who have been forced to seek supplementary assistance from the National Insurance Institute has recently been reported. According to research carried out in 1986, 65 percent of workers in the clothing industry were low paid (defined as those earning below the minimum wage, equal to 35 percent of average earnings) and accounted for 30 percent of all industrial workers on low earnings. In the leather industry the figure for low earners was 48 percent, in textiles 45 percent, and in food 40 percent. The rise in real wages was less in these industries than in most others. Interindustry differentials explain more than half the inequality in wages.[14] Low wages are also a significant cause of poverty (see Chapter 8).

Indexation and Wage Policy

The Histadrut in the first twenty years of its existence, in an economy controlled by the British Mandatory Authorities, was mainly concerned with preventing the wages of unskilled Jewish labor from being undercut by cheaper Arab labor. After the Second World War the Histadrut's bargaining power increased; centralized wage agreements were negotiated with the government and, as will be seen, there was no downward pressure on wages from Arab labor.

One of the most important ways in which wages have been increased is through the system of indexation that began in the prestate period. The Mandatory government used the cost-of-living allowance to compensate employees for inflation, thus avoiding disputes with its employees. The system was inherited by the Israeli government in 1948.

The War of Independence resulted in the exodus of many Arabs from areas that became part of Israel. They no longer served as a competitive threat to unskilled Jewish labor. Immigration rapidly increased the labor supply, particularly of unskilled workers. Attempts were made to freeze wages in order to reduce inflation but these had little success. In the late 1950s linkage had the effect of fixing the differentials between the wages of different groups of workers. In an attempt to modify the system, a public committee was set up in the mid-1960s with the aim of protecting the share of wages in national income rather than its absolute value. This idea was not implemented, however.

In 1975 full indexation was replaced by partial cost-of-living compensation agreements and national wage deals. The terms of these arrangements changed continuously, but typically the Histadrut and the Employers' Federation would negotiate an agreement whereby between 70 percent and 90 percent of the increase in the consumer price index per month would be paid in compensation to employees in the following month. The Minister of Labor then issues an extension order obliging all employers to pay the cost-of-living allowance. This sum is paid on top of wage increases negotiated on an industry basis between the Histadrut and the Manufacturers' Association and in plant negotiations on individual rates.

Shares of Labor and Capital in National Income

The increase in the share of labor in national income has brought with it a fall in that of capital. Between 1971 and 1975 the average share of labor was 72 percent, that of capital 28 percent. In the period 1977–1982 labor's share came to 83 percent and between 1983 and 1985 to 88.3 percent. In 1989 it was 87 percent.[15] This change represented a 2 percent fall from 1986 and resulted from the recession in the economy and the resulting rise in unemployment. The share of labor includes earnings of the owners of small companies, and allowing for this reduces the share of labor in 1989 to about 80 percent. The share of capital includes nonwage payments: the earnings of the self-employed and of those in cooperatives. Despite these adjustments the trend is clear: The share of labor rose by about 17 percent between the period 1971–1975 and 1989. The lower levels of profitability that this rise caused discouraged investment and restricted growth of the business sector. The mechanisms behind the high and increasing share of labor have been, until recently, the indexation of wages and low levels of unemployment.

The increase in the share of labor in national income has been accompanied by a growing inequality in the distribution of incomes from earnings (see Chapter 8). Growing inequality has not resulted from the increased profitability of capital but from a redistribution between workers in favor of higher earners.

Conclusion

There are several major problems in the labor market that affect the economy as a whole. The first is the large share of workers in the public sector. The second is the relatively low participation rate in the labor force. These two factors combine to restrict the supply of labor to the productive sectors of the economy. The relationship between the cost of labor and net earnings has been subject to much debate and attempts have made to reduce the wide gap by cutting employers' national contribution and reducing income tax.

The increased share of labor in the national income has not come about as a result of ideological strength in the Labor movement. In fact the movement's sense of purpose and its popularity have declined at the same time as its major industrial holdings have run into serious economic decline. The movement has failed to articulate a new or renewed policy for the mixed economy at a time when the existing policies have been badly affected by changes in the economy.

Near full employment, which prevailed until recently, and the indexation system have helped to push up the share of labor in national income. Income inequalities have grown and the social pressures that these have created are a major factor behind the large social welfare budgets that are examined in the next chapter.

Notes

1. Y. Ben Porath, *Patterns and Peculiarities of Economic Growth and Structure* (Jerusalem: Falk Institute, 1986).

2. E. Kleiman, "The Histadrut Economy of Israel: In Search of Criteria," *Jerusalem Quarterly*, no. 41 (Winter 1987).

3. *Ha'aretz* (Tel Aviv), 21 June 1990. In Hebrew.

4. H. Barkai, *Kibbutz Efficiency and the Incentive Conundrum* (Jerusalem: Falk Institute, 1987).

5. W. Preuss, *The Labour Market in Israel* (Jerusalem: Rubin Mass, 1961), and *Statistical Abstract of Israel 1989* (Jerusalem: Central Bureau of Statistics, 1989).

6. *Report of the Palestine Royal Commission* (London: Her Majesty's Stationery Office, 1937), Command number 5479, Chapter 1, p. 13.

7. Y. Ben Porath, *The Entwined Growth of Population and Product 1922–1982* (Jerusalem: Falk Institute Paper, May 1985).

8. Quoted in *Davar* (Tel Aviv), 31 March 1987. In Hebrew.

9. Y. Ben Porath, "Diversity in Population and the Labor Force," in Y. Ben Porath, ed., *The Israeli Economy: Maturing Through Crises* (Cambridge, Mass.: Harvard University Press, 1986).

10. S. Amir, "Educational Structure and Wage Levels," in Y. Ben Porath, ed., *The Israeli Economy: Maturing Through Crises.*

11. Porath, "Diversity in Population and the Labor Force."

12. R. Klinov-Malul, *Israel's Changing Industrial Structure: Years of Growth and Years of Slowdown* (Jerusalem: Falk Institute Paper, December 1984).

13. "Labor Force Statistics," *Economic Outlook Papers* (Paris: Organization for Economic Cooperation and Development, May 1986); *Monthly Bulletin of Statistics* (Jerusalem: Central Bureau of Statistics, May 1985) and Press Release (Jerusalem: Central Bureau of Statistics, December 1986).

14. G. Weinblatt and I. Luski, *Structure of Salaries in Industry and the Ramifications of Implementing a Minimum Wage* (Jerusalem: Israel Center for Social Policy Research, January 1987). In Hebrew.

15. *Annual Report* (Tel Aviv: Institute for Research on Ouput and Incomes, 1975, 1981, 1984, 1985, and 1989). In Hebrew.

8

The Public Sector: The Role of the Government and the Social Services

The Role of the Government

The public sector plays a dominant role in the Israeli economy: Its expenditures equal about 65 percent of gross national product (GNP). It consists of central and local government, national organizations such as the Jewish Agency, the education sector, the National Insurance Institute (NII), hospitals, and the health funds as well as other non–profit making bodies. Its expenditures as a share of national income fell by about 9 percent since the early 1980s.

Although the volume of public expenditure is not the only guide to the strength of government intervention in the economy, it is the most easily quantifiable. The main forms of central government expenditure are examined in this chapter and the activities of some major nongovernmental bodies are looked at from an institutional viewpoint.

The largest financial contributor in the public sector is the central government. Largely as a result of the 1985 stabilization program, government expenditures grew more slowly in the period 1985–1988 than they did in the previous five years. This trend was less marked for the public sector as a whole. Government revenues increased more quickly after 1985 than did those of the public sector (see Tables 8.1 and 8.2).

Government Expenditure

One of the most important features of the economy during the last twenty years has been the growth of government expenditure. In 1960 total public expenditure equalled 29 percent of GNP; in 1985 it reached a peak of 65.2 percent.[1] Figure 8.1 shows the main trends in government expenditure since 1980. The share of civilian consumption and investment fell while that of debt repayment rose dramatically. Despite the Lebanon war, the share of defense also declined, as did that of transfers. The impact

TABLE 8.1
Income, Expenditure, and Deficits of the Public Sector, 1980-1988
(percentage of GNP, current prices)

	1980-1984	1985-1988
Total public spending	72.8	65.6
Domestic	61.2	54.8
Abroad	11.6	10.8
Total income	58.4	63.9
Domestic	48.3	50.1
taxes & transfers from the public	43.2	46.5
property income	2.8	2.6
Foreign	10.1	13.8
Deficit (minus)/surplus	-14.4	-1.7
Domestic	-12.9	-4.7
Foreign	-1.5	3.0
Financing the deficit		
Foreign loans	6.5	-0.2
Net printing of money	1.8	0.3
Internal loans	2.4	-2.2
Residual	3.6	3.7
Public Sector Debt		
Internal	121.4	119.6
External	40.2	37.8

Source: Annual Report 1988, Jerusalem: Bank of Israel, 1989.

of the cuts in civilian consumption on the education and health systems is examined in separate sections below.

Table 8.2 shows how reductions in government expenditure were concentrated on domestic expenditures: As a share of GNP they fell from 49 percent in the period 1982–1984 to 42.8 percent in the period 1985–1988. In July 1985 U.S. aid increased, making it possible to maintain high levels of defense imports. Local revenues increased from 40.6 percent in the period 1982–1984 to 41.6 percent in the period 1985–1988, but from

TABLE 8.2
Central Government Income, Expenditure, and Deficit, 1982-1988
(percentage of GNP, budget years)

	1982-1984	1985-1988
Total spending	63.0	55.1
Local	49.0	42.8
Abroad	14.0	12.2
Total income	51.1	55.2
Local	40.6	41.4
Abroad	10.5	13.8
Deficit (minus)/surplus	12.0	2.1
Local	-8.4	-1.2
Abroad	-3.5	1.6
Financing the deficit (minus)/surplus	12.0	-0.2
Local capital raised	3.8	2.8
Foreign loans	8.1	0.5
Bank of Israel	0	-2.2

Source: Annual Report 1988, Jerusalem: Bank of Israel, 1989.

1985 to 1988 the increase in revenue was used to reduce the budget deficit rather than increase domestic expenditure. The government and its economic advisers considered taxation and expenditure too high. Therefore, they aimed to balance the budget by increasing taxation temporarily and cutting expenditure permanently. Since 1988 expenditures have increased again and taxation remains high, if not at its 1986 level.

The state budget has two parts: the current or ordinary budget and the development budget. The ordinary budget covers current expenditures on goods and services, interest payments on the national debt, and the reserve. The development budget covers transfers to the private sector, social and economic investment, and repayments of debt capital (see Figure 8.1 for trends in government expenditure).

The central government, as well as carrying out its own direct expenditures, transfers funds to cover part of the expenditure of local authorities,

Figure 8.1 Government Expenditure by Type, 1980-1991

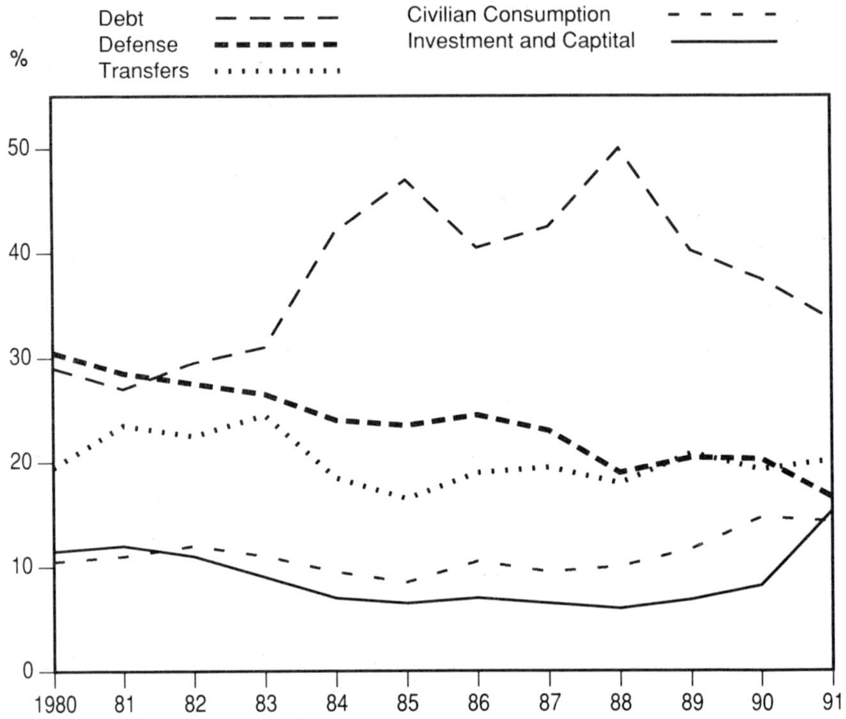

Source: Main Points of the Budget 1982-1991, Ministry of Finance

public corporations, health funds, and other non–profit making organizations included in the public sector.

Table 8.3 provides a breakdown of the 1991 budget. The budget was issued for the first nine months of 1991. If the officially estimated exchange rate for the period is used, it is possible to make crude estimates of the annual volume of expenditure in dollar terms. Total expenditure is planned at $40 billion, of which defense accounts for $6.4 bn., debt repayment $13.7 bn., welfare payments $3.9 bn., reserves $1.8 bn., central government administration $1.2 bn., state pensions $800 million, and credit subsidies $300 million. This leaves a discretionary amount of $11.9 bn. over which the government had some leeway for decision making.

The most important feature of the 1991 budget is the increased allocation to investment (the share of total expenditure devoted to investment is nearly double that in the 1990 budget), designed to help the economy absorb the large number of new immigrants. The budget contains provi-

TABLE 8.3
The 1991 State Budget

	Shekels (billions)	Percent
Expenditure		
Total	66.5	100.0
Current	45.2	68.0
administration	3.4	5.1
defense	10.7	16.0
education	4.6	6.9
welfare and labor	6.4	8.3
other social services	2.5	4.0
immigrant absorption	1.2	1.8
health	0.7	1.1
food and agricultural subsidies	0.7	1.1
economic services	1.1	1.7
credit subsidy	0.5	0.7
local authorities	0.8	1.2
interest	9.7	14.4
reserves	2.9	4.4
Development and capital	21.3	29.6
investment in the economy	1.8	2.7
investment in social services	6.0	9.0
debt repayment	11.6	17.5
local authorities	0.3	0.4
Repayment of debt to Bank of Israel	1.6	2.4
Revenue		
Total	66.5	100.0
Current	45.2	68.0
direct tax	17.4	26.2
indirect tax	17.7	26.6
interest and profits	1.2	1.8
transfers from capital account	8.9	13.4
Loans and capital	19.7	29.6
Loans from Bank of Israel	1.6	2.4

Source: Main Points of the Budget 1991. Jerusalem: Ministry of Finance, 1990.

sions to build 70,000 apartments and to provide up to 100,000 temporary homes in army bases, kibbutzim, and hotels. Mortgages will be provided to 35,000 families. The government will provide 1.3 billion shekels in welfare benefits and will spend 400 million shekels providing 40,000 old age pensions for new immigrants.

As a result of the increased allocations for immigrant absorption, total expenditure in current prices is expected to rise by 23 percent. This figure compares to a forecast rise in prices of 19 percent. Although revenues are expected to rise (both as a result of faster economic growth and because of higher taxation), the budget deficit is forecast at about 7 percent of gross domestic product (GDP), at least 2 percent higher than in 1990.

Subsidies

Subsidies play an important role in the economy, despite major cuts in 1985. They have a number of different functions: to promote welfare; encourage investment, employment, and exports; and balance growth regionally.

The government subsidizes some basic foods in order to reduce the cost of living for the poor. As all consumers benefit, these kinds of subsidies have been cut drastically in the last five years. Education and health are also subsidized, as is public transport. There are debates about the advantages of these kinds of subsidies, but there is a consensus on their public provision.

Subsidies designed to encourage investment are the subject of much scrutiny at present. The theory behind this type of expenditure is that at an early stage of economic development private entrepreneurs may not want or be able to take risks, given the level of uncertainty about the way in which the economy will develop. Only the government can give a sense of direction and provide some of the financial means to take such risks. This rationale is used in support of subsidies for investment in plants and equipment as well as for research and development.

Other types of subsidies have been developed in Israel for a wide range of reasons. One of the most important reasons, in the early 1980s, was the desire to avoid the direct effects of inflation: Rather than raise prices explicitly the government provided a subsidy. As the shekel's rate of exchange has frequently been overvalued (devaluations have not matched the difference between inflation rates in Israel and those in its trading partners), the government has "subsidized" exports. Exchange rate insurance is designed to protect exporters from the effects of inflation. Exchange rate insurance in effect provides an alternative exchange rate for exporters. It thus protects a particular group from the effects of economic policy and

TABLE 8.4
Subsidies and Grants to the Business Sector, 1980-1990

	Percent of business sector GDP	Percent of GDP
1980	16.7	11.5
1981	21.3	14.6
1982	17.0	11.7
1983	15.7	10.7
1984	15.6	10.5
1985	11.3	7.8
1986	7.9	5.6
1987	7.7	5.5
1988	8.2	5.8
1989	7.1	4.9
1990	6.6	4.6

Definitions: Business sector GDP is defined as equal to that of the whole economy minus the output of housing, government and of non-profit making organizations services.
Subsidies are defined as all grants on current account by central and local governments to private industry and public corporations and the operational deficits of government enterprises. Also included are capital grants and loan subsidies.

Sources: Monthly Bulletin of Statistics, Supplements, Jerusalem: Central Bureau of Statistics, May 1988, May 1990 and May 1991.

is designed to maintain exports in an environment that would discourage them if the subsidy did not exist.

Table 8.4 shows the very high level of subsidies reached in 1981 and the major cuts enacted in 1985. In 1981 the volume of subsidies reached a peak at about $3.8 billion; in 1989 it was about $2 billion.

Subsidies listed in the state budget give only a partial picture of the total volume. The government also uses indirect methods to subsidize certain firms. These practices may result in a serious waste of resources, but they also hide the subsidies from the public view and from the legislature. Many of them cannot be easily quantified. The extent of overemployment in the public sector has never been precisely calculated, although it can be considered a form of subsidized employment.

Interest on many of the loans to industry was not linked to the consumer price index or the exchange rate during the period of accelerating inflation up to 1979 and thus was, in effect, heavily subsidized. These subsidies were mainly granted to firms located in development areas, where the government tried to encourage industrial development. The 1990 budget allocated 550 million shekels for subsidizing loans made before 1985. The government replaced loans with capital grants for 38 percent of the cost of investment in equipment. The 1990 grant allocation was 210 million shekels. Total grants in the 1990 budget came to about 2.2 billion shekels, or about $970 million, at the officially estimated rate of exchange for the fiscal year. This figure excludes subsidies included in Table 8.4.

To these subsidies should be added a series of tax benefits that effectively subsidize different groups in the economy. In the 1990 budget they totalled 5.43 billion shekels and included reduced rates of income, value added, travel, corporation, and purchase taxes as well as customs duties. This very broad definition of the level of subsidies brings us to a figure of 7.16 billion shekels, nearly 6 percent of GDP. (The GDP estimate is for calendar year 1990; the budget figures are for April 1, 1990 to March 31, 1991.)

Subsidies are not directed to one overall aim; they contributed to the budget deficit, the financing of which resulted in controlled capital markets, which in turn made directed credit necessary. It also means that politico-bureaucratic decisions and controls play a central role in the economy, with very serious costs in efficiency terms.

Government Revenues

Government expenditure is funded by taxation, by borrowing at home and abroad (examined in Chapters 2 and 6), and by revenues earned on government assets and through taxation. The largest source of revenues is taxation.

Taxation

The Israeli tax system incorporates almost every form of tax that the ingenuity of man can devise.[2] Although the declared policy of the state has been to raise taxes equitably and to avoid excess taxes, which would harm productivity and production, Israelis are among the most highly taxed people in the world. In 1986 taxes took 46 percent of GDP, compared with 28.5 percent in the United States, 40.6 percent in West Germany, and 52.9 percent in Sweden.[3]

Figure 8.2 gives an indication of how the burden of taxation has risen. In the years 1981 to 1985 total tax and transfers from the public to the

Figure 8.2 The Tax Burden in Israel: Total Taxation Minus Subsidies and Transfers as Percentage of GNP, 1960-1989

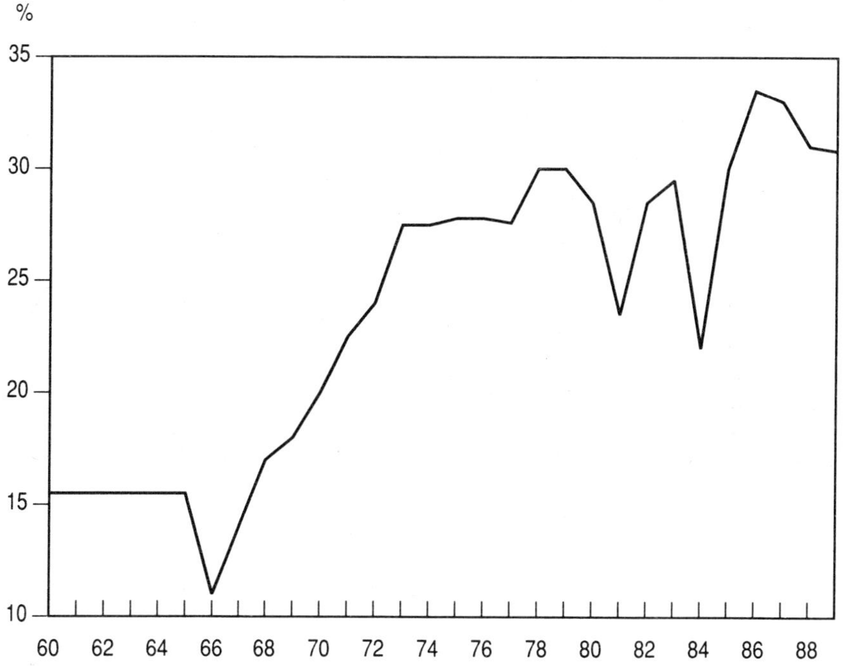

Source: Ministry of Finance, Main Points of the Budget 1989

government (excluding those on property) rose by the equivalent of 4 percent of GNP. The net amount, after allowing for transfer payments that the government makes to the public, rose by 6 percent of GNP. The breakdown of government revenues in the 1991 budget is given in Table 8.3.

In 1988 a government-appointed commission recommended major income tax reforms. Its main proposal was to reduce the burden of income tax by increasing tax bands and reducing tax rates. This reform was to be financed by ending tax concessions granted to many groups, such as immigrants and residents of development towns, and by taxing all benefits given to workers. The most important of these are employers' contributions to training funds and savings schemes, including pensions, which are currently not taxed. They tend to benefit the better paid more than those on average or below average earnings. The report recognized that many disincentives and inequities had crept into the taxation and payments systems since the major reform of 1975. The 1990 budget implementated part of the reform proposals.

The complexity of the tax system is now part of Israel's folklore. The 1962 Income Tax Ordinance had 244 sections in twelve chapters; the 1987 customs duty and sales tax guide was 697 pages long, listing at least thirty rates of duty and ten rates of tax. The 1989 budget listed revenues from nine income and property taxes and charges, as well as from eleven forms of indirect taxes. Government ministries administer seventy other charges. Each tax, especially that on income, has its inevitable complications, designed to prevent avoidance and to cope with inflation. Firms cannot get advanced rulings on what the tax treatment of various activities will be. "One-off" taxes are frequently repeated and tax rates are changed continuously, which makes planning extremely difficult.

Israel is under pressure from the United States and the European Community to reduce its taxes on imports and the travel tax paid by Israeli residents on journeys abroad. The effects of the free trade agreements will increasingly be felt in the liberalization of the tax system.

Publicly Owned Land

In addition to all the controls and influence that the government has, it owns or is responsible for the management of just over 90 percent of the land in Israel. The complexity of the current pattern of land ownership has its origins in the prestate period when Jews all over the world contributed funds for the purchase of land in Palestine. This land was to be used for the Jewish people as a whole, and the official institutions of Palestine's Jewish community used the land so purchased for development. In 1961 this land, together with that owned by the government (which was inherited from the British Mandatory Authorities) and land plus buildings abandoned by Arab refugees during the War of Independence, was placed in the hands of a new government body, the Israel Lands Administration (ILA). Part of the agreement between the Jewish National Fund (owners of land bought by Diaspora Jews) and the government stated that the ILA would not sell land, except in special circumstances and in very small quantities. All the land would be leased for periods of forty-nine years (based on a biblical precept that was adopted by the fund), and then leased again for a further forty-nine years. This condition is true of nearly all land held by the ILA for residential, industrial, and agricultural purposes.

A large portion of residential land is publicly owned. Many residents are, therefore, leaseholders and are subject to various charges and bureaucratic restrictions administered by the ILA, in addition to the planning regulations of local authorities. The ILA makes available small amounts of land on a leased basis each year to the Ministry of Housing, the mortgage banks, and to private builders. The limited nature of these releases has been a major factor behind high and rising housing costs. The ILA has approximately 400,000 leaseholders.

Privatization

In recent years the negative impact of large-scale government ownership and intervention has been increasingly recognized in official and other circles. As a result, the sale of government-owned companies to the private sector has been official policy for the last fifteen years but little has been achieved. In 1988 the First Boston Corporation of the United States issued a report, commissioned by the Ministry of Finance's Government Corporations Authority, on privatization: the selling of government-owned businesses. It proposed to sell, by different means, a large group of government companies including Israel Chemical Industries, Bezek (Israel Telecommunications), Israel Electric Corporation, El Al Israel Airlines, Israel Aircraft Industries, Elta, Oil Refineries, Ltd., and Zim Navigation.

The government's objectives were to reduce its involvement in the economy and the pressure on its budget, to increase the role of the market, to develop the capital market, to encourage foreign investment, and to free these companies from government restraints. The revenues were to be used to reduce the government's debt. Four groups of investors were identified: the labor force of these companies (about 65,000), institutions such as provident funds and insurance companies, private companies, and the general public. Another advantage of privatization was the depoliticization of the boards of directors and managements of these companies. There is, however, no theoretical reason why these firms could not be made more commercial with the increased profits benefitting the public as a whole. In the Israeli context, freeing companies from political appointments by ministers would yield considerable benefits. Privatization has occurred in fits and starts where government ministers have been able to agree. There is no clear program, however, to which the government as a whole is committed. So far 75 percent of the shares of the Paz oil company and 82 percent of those of the Jerusalem Economic Corporation have been privatized. Along with shares in a number of smaller companies, about $300 million has been raised.[4]

Broader Aspects of Government Intervention in the Economy

In addition to the monetary and fiscal measures and its control of the foreign exchange rate, the government has a large number of other means to influence economic activity. It controls the prices charged by many companies and it influences wages, not only as a large employer, but also by issuing extension orders to agreements reached between the Histadrut and the Manufacturers' (employers') Association. These orders require all employers to pay cost-of-living adjustments.

The government issues licenses for most business activities and imports. It may limit competition by administrative order (for example, by banning charter flights, as it did between 1963 and 1977) or by not granting a license to a new competitor. It also maintains administrative controls on numerous activities.

The government also assists a number of industries and firms on an ad hoc basis. In some cases, it uses its procurement power to help certain firms or acquires shares in firms in order to rescue them from bankruptcy. Elsewhere the government takes upon itself business risks, including those resulting from bad management. It guarantees procurement of total production at an agreed price, or on cost-plus arrangements in the defense sector. It helps industry in general terms: directing credits, guaranteeing loans, granting tax exemptions, and subsidizing fixed assets and research and development, especially at universities and research institutes. It also regulates mergers. In recent years, it has become aware of the problems faced by Israeli firms in marketing their products abroad and has started to provide assistance in this regard.

The government also controls (and subsidizes) various input prices: oil was supplied, transported, and sold by a cartel of three firms, subject to price controls until recently. Beginning in 1957, an equalization fund for oil prices was used to subsidize certain energy prices and purchases by the Israel Electric Corporation. In 1988 reforms in this sector were introduced but they were much less radical than those initially proposed. Water is also subject to central control, quota allocations, and subsidies at different rates to agriculture, industry, and other areas. The government imports meat, soya, and fodder itself. It also owns and controls the water distribution system, something that was examined in Chapter 4. As a result of this vast array of tools, business firms are very dependent on government.

Social Services

Israel has a mixed economy with a strong tradition of providing social services by public means. In this respect it is ideologically closer to Western European countries than to the United States. The welfare state provides health, education, and welfare services, financed by taxation and earnings-related contributions. The services provided are far from complete and are often below the acceptable standard.

There are two types of social services expenditures: those on welfare payments and those on services such as health and education. Increased real expenditures on welfare benefits have not prevented the spread of poverty, and there are anxieties that education and health services are so overburdened in some areas that they are not functioning properly.

Welfare payments have, since 1980, risen in line with the increase in population. Overall social services spending has been largely frozen, and so per capita expenditure has fallen. Between 1980 and 1989, government spending on social services rose by 34 percent, from 8.3 billion shekels (1988/89 prices) in 1980 to a planned 11.1 billion shekels in 1989 (1988/89 prices). This growth resulted in an increase in the share of the budget for social services from 18–23 percent in the period 1985–1988 to 30 percent in 1991.

The increase in transfer payments (pensions, unemployment benefits, and other welfare payments) paid through the National Insurance Institute was 80 percent. Expenditure on education, health, and personal social services rose by only 8 percent. As a share of GNP, transfers increased from 5.4 percent to 7.5 percent while services fell from 9.7 percent to 8.6 percent.[5]

The government is trying to reverse the trend, partly in order to improve public services and also because increased immigration has pushed up demand for them. High unemployment makes it harder, however, to reduce benefits paid through the national insurance.

Education

The main trends affecting demand for expenditure on education in recent years result from changes in the age structure of the population. There has been an increase in post–primary school enrollment, but no significant increase in primary school enrollment, and expenditure there has been reduced. Kindergartens, which are compulsory for five year olds, saw a small increase in expenditure.

National expenditure on education in real terms grew by 4.5 percent between 1970 and 1974 and by 7 percent between 1974 and 1979. In 1980–1984 it actually fell by an average of 0.5 percent a year and between 1986 and 1989 is estimated to have increased by 2.6 percent annually.

Cuts in the education budget have resulted in a reduction of school hours; financially well-off parents have increasingly supplemented their children's school education with private lessons. The cuts have also resulted in many classes of over forty pupils per teacher. It is also recognized that teachers are so badly paid that many potentially good ones do not go into the profession. There is growing concern about the quality of education and the level of educational achievement.

Despite these problems educational achievement (measured quantitatively in Table 7.1) increased, which was true even between 1985 and

1989. There has been a continuous increase in the share of the population receiving longer periods of school education. As was noted in Chapter 7, severe inequalities between different communities remain, and these figures say little about qualitative achievement.

The 1990 budget contained proposals for the reintroduction of a long school day. Cuts in hours of education have resulted in most schools providing classes for half a day. This practice not only encouraged private education in the afternoons, which the poor could not afford, but restricted the ability of parents to work; they had to collect their children from school in the middle of the day. The cost of increasing school hours was largely to be covered by charges paid by parents according to their income and the number of children they have in school. At the end of 1991 these proposals had not been implemented.

The higher education system includes six universities with about 80,000 students. There is concern about the quality of education, the provision of basic services (such as books), and the level of research, both applied and theoretical. Budgets have been cut, students' fees have been increased, and most of the universities have run into financial difficulties. They received about 62 percent of their authorized budget from the central government in the years 1986 and 1987. All of the universities have extensive fund-raising organizations in Israel and abroad, which play an important role in financing capital projects but do not cover current costs such as salaries. There are, therefore, serious imbalances within their budgets: Funds are often available for new buildings but not for books.

The Everyman's University, modelled on the United Kingdom's Open University, has 20,000 full- and part-time students who study at home using radio and television courses. Although it was set up with funds from the Rothschild family and continues to receive assistance from that source, it is part of the national higher education system.

Health

Israel has a system of socialized medicine based on collective health insurance. All those who work contribute to a health fund of their choice (as do their employers) and the government pays the contribution of those receiving welfare payments.

The health funds also provide medical facilities, principally clinics. The largest of them, the Histadrut's Kupat Holim Clalit, also runs hospitals and other facilities. The functions of the health funds overlap with those of the government, which itself runs a network of hospitals. There is a serious lack of coordination and cooperation within the system and the resulting duplication of services is wasteful. Strong trade unions for doctors, nurses, and hospital workers have also complicated the management of the system. Different groups have constantly battled for their own interests and as a result the whole service has suffered. One consequence is that Israel has no general hospitals: Each hospital is a special center, often with prestigious facilities, created without a national plan.

Finance is provided by the government, employers, and employees through the National Insurance Institute and also through voluntary contributions. Kupat Holim Clalit has been unwilling to increase its membership contributions in recent years out of fear that it will lose members to the smaller, more dynamic funds that offer a slightly less comprehensive range of services. It is, therefore, in severe economic difficulties and suffers constant problems in its operations. The Histadrut's health fund receives financial support from the government, but there is a constant conflict over the amount to be paid. On the one hand, the government has often demanded limitations of services and increased charges by the fund. On the other hand, the health fund has complained of being underfunded. In 1986/87 Kupat Holim Clalit's income was 1.2 billion shekels, 10 percent of which was passed onto the Histadrut for other activities. It employed 22,500 workers and had an accumulated debt of $525 million.[6]

The largest single element in health expenditure is the government-controlled National Insurance Institute's contribution to the health funds. This contribution is financed by a so-called "parallel tax" collected from employers. Although this amount has grown, the government's own allocation to health has been cut in real terms in recent years. The health funds receive proceeds of the parallel tax in addition to the membership fees that they levy themselves. There is, therefore, an expensive duplication in the collection of funds: The NII collects funds (which in some other countries is done by the income tax authorities), as do the health funds. Each organization maintains a large staff to handle this function and none is willing to trust the others to raise the funds for them.

The government is responsible for the running of state-owned hospitals, mental hospitals, and long-term-care facilities. The national hospital service has been expanded due to a growing and aging population. More money has been spent on expensive intensive care and on cheaper day care. There is no national dental care service. The health service is characterized by very high use of clinics, with up to ten visits per patient each year compared to an average of 4.23 in the Organization for Economic Cooperation and Development (OECD) countries.[7] The government is, therefore, trying to introduce charges for appointments with doctors.

In 1983 the government funded 57 percent of health expenditure; in the 1991 budget plan its contribution was 42 percent. The balance came from the membership fees paid to the health funds, which are non–profit making organizations (NPOs).[8]

The most important NPO is Kupat Holim Clalit, which provides health services for about 80 percent of the population. There are two other, smaller funds that cover the rest of the population. One major hospital and the national ambulance service are semi-independent charities with substantial foreign funding.

As a result of the different controlling interests in the health services there is a complicated financial system designed to cover costs: For example, a health fund will pay for hospital facilities used by its members; patients constantly have to deal with paperwork in order to ensure that one body will pay the other on their behalf.

There are also strong pressures to bring private medicine into the public hospitals. Higher pay for hospital doctors is a precondition for easing these pressures. Reform is contingent on a willingness to put sectoral interests aside in favor of those of the system as a whole. In this respect the problems of the health services are a microcosm of those of the economy as a whole.

Welfare

Increased spending on welfare has been a major source of pressure on total public expenditure. Transfers from the government to individuals increased from 5.5 percent of GNP in 1960 to 8.4 percent in 1970, with a peak of about 18 percent in 1983.

The main source of transfer payments is the NII, which collects payments from employers and employees; it also receives funds directly from the government. It distributes a wide range of transfer payments, including retirement and old age pensions, as well as allowances to families with low incomes and to those with sons in the army. It also pays the salaries of reservists while they are on military duty. In 1990 payments made by the NII were budgeted at 7.2 billion shekels. The government finances part of the NII's expenditure; in the 1990 budget plan nearly 4.5 billion shekels was allocated for this purpose. The volume of benefits that the NII paid has risen, but since 1981 contributions to the NII have not been enough to cover the deficit in its budget; for this reason, the government has contributed funds. Benefits paid by the NII came to 2.8 percent of GNP in 1970, 6.75 percent in 1980, and an estimated 8 percent in 1987.[9]

Not only did the burden on the state budget increase, but, over a much longer period, contributions also have risen as a share of wages, salaries, and the income of the self-employed. In 1954 the share of employees' wages paid by the employee and employer to the NII was 5.45 percent. In 1979 it reached a peak of 21.5 percent; by 1991 the share had fallen to 14.7 percent.[10] Between 1976 and 1980 national insurance payments on wages by employers and employees were equal to more than 90 percent of the income tax collected on wages. In 1986 they came to 86 percent.

In the 1991 budget the major elements in NII expenditure were child allowances (19 percent), old age pensions and related payments (37 percent), and unemployment benefits (6 percent).[11]

Beginning in 1975, when there was a major tax/benefit reform, the NII paid allowances for all children. Tax exemptions for parents were withdrawn. Child allowances were cancelled for the first child in 1985. In 1987 they were restored for families earning less than 90 percent of the average wage. In 1990 allowances for the second child in all families with up to three children and an income exceeding 120 percent of the national average were withdrawn. The number of households receiving child allowances fell from 580,000 in 1980 to 540,000 in 1989. The 1990 budget also changed the linkage system for old age pensions so as to reduce their cost.

The NII paid old age pensions to 343,000 individuals in 1980 and to 418,000 in 1988. It paid unemployment benefits to 37,000 people in 1980 and to 93,000 in 1988. Benefits of other kinds were paid to 160,000 individuals in 1980 and to 190,000 in 1988. This, together with the increase in the number of pensioners, represented an 11 percent increase in its total caseload.[12]

The Government's Role in Reducing Income Inequality

Income Distribution

In 1971 a commission set up to investigate the distribution of income and social inequality reported that the former had become more equal in the years leading up to its report.[13] This change meant that the poorer sections of society increased their share of total income while the richer sections received relatively less. This process continued until 1975; after that time, inequality increased and by 1984 was nearly as great as it had been seventeen years earlier. The reduction of inequality and the number of people living in poverty in the mid-1970s was the result of full employment, increasing social security transfers, and the improved educational level of the population.[14]

The two most recent surveys of family expenditure patterns were carried out in 1979/80 and in 1986/77. These surveys are more comprehensive than annual income surveys and form the basis of the comparisons made below in respect to the distribution of income and the level of poverty. The quality of the 1986/87 survey was much lower than the 1979/80 survey and so only general conclusions can be drawn about the trends during that period. According to the NII, there was little significant change in either the distribution of income or the level of poverty between 1986/87 and 1988, when the most recently published income survey came out.

Table 8.5 shows that there was an increase in the inequality of earned income as indicated by a rise in the Gini coefficient from 0.43 in 1979/80 to 0.46 in 1986/87. (The Gini coefficient can be simply defined as a measure of the difference between absolute equality in the distribution of income and the existing distribution.) The Gini coefficient for gross income increased from 0.36 to 0.38. Gross incomes are those from earnings and from national insurance benefits. The Gini coefficient for net income (after tax as well as transfers from national insurance) changed little. Thus transfers and taxes did more to reduce inequality in 1986/87 than they did eight years earlier, but there was more inequality to reduce. Increased inequality in the distribution of income before transfers and taxes was in part caused by a rise in unemployment from 3.2 percent of the labor force in 1979/80 to 6.2 percent in 1986/87.

Poverty

In order to reduce, or at least alleviate, the extent of poverty, the government spent increasing amounts on transfer payments to maintain income. These payments consisted of child, maternity, old age, and disability allowances paid by the NII as well as other payments designed to supplement the incomes of those receiving low pay.

Transfer payments were not designed to change the distribution of income but rather to reduce the level of poverty. The latter is officially measured in a relative way. Those whose income is 40 percent below the median income in the economy are considered poor. The median income is that which 50 percent of the population earn more than and 50 percent earn less than. Hence, the poverty line changes as the median income does. In the past ten years, real incomes have risen and, thus, the median income has as well; as a result, the income of those on the poverty line has increased in real terms.

Table 8.6 provides data on the extent of poverty in the population as a whole. It shows that in the eight years to 1986/87 the percentage of families whose earnings, before taxes and benefits, left them in poverty rose from 24.7 percent to 27.8 percent. These figures show the effect of the earnings system on the level of poverty. When benefits are added, the number in poverty was 13.2 percent in 1979/80 and 10.6 percent in 1986/87. When taxes are deducted, one sees a fall from 16 percent in 1979/80 to 12.3 percent in 1986/87. In absolute terms the number of families in poverty, on the basis of their net income, rose as the size of the population did. In 1986/87, 134,516 families, comprising 633,810 people, lived in poverty.

TABLE 8.5
The Distribution of Income of the Whole Population, 1979/1980 and 1986/1987

	Share of each decile in total income (percentage) [a]					
	Income before transfers and taxes		Income after transfers		Income after transfers and taxes	
Decile	1979/80	1986/87	1979/80	1986/87	1979/80	1986/87
1st	0.52	0.10	2.53	2.56	3.31	3.19
2nd	2.70	2.14	3.80	3.74	4.61	4.56
3rd	4.19	3.75	4.84	4.74	5.54	5.56
4th	5.54	5.11	5.89	5.77	6.58	6.60
5th	7.06	6.73	7.21	7.05	7.82	7.83
6th	8.86	8.14	8.76	8.46	9.21	9.12
7th	11.05	10.59	10.65	10.16	10.79	10.69
8th	13.78	13.34	13.03	12.50	12.78	12.66
9th	17.42	17.89	16.36	16.35	15.42	15.67
Top	28.87	31.80	26.94	28.67	23.94	24.12
Ratio of incomes in top and bottom deciles	55.5	318	10.6	11.2	7.2	7.6
Gini coefficient	0.425	0.461	0.364	0.378	0.312	0.315

[a] Not all columns total 100 due to rounding.

Source: Annual Survey 1987, Jerusalem: National Insurance Institute, 1988.

TABLE 8.6
Poverty in the Urban Population, 1979/1980 and 1986/1987

	Before transfers and taxes		After transfers		After transfers and taxes	
	1979/80	1986/87	1979/80	1986/87	1979/80	1986/87
Percentage in poverty:						
Families	24.7	27.8	13.2	10.6	16.0	12.3
Individuals [a]	23.0	27.8	12.8	13.7	17.5	16.6
Children	22.5	30.9	13.5	17.3	20.5	21.5
Number in poverty:						
Families	n.a.	303,968	n.a.	115,391	n.a.	134,516
Individuals [a]	n.a.	1,063,112	n.a.	523,922	n.a.	633,810
Children	n.a.	451,713	n.a.	253,270	n.a.	314,980

[a] Adults and children
Changes in the definition of urban areas makes comparisons between 1979/80 and 1986/87 possible only in general terms.
n.a. = not available

Source: Annual Survey 1987, Jerusalem: National Insurance Institute, 1988.

The official poverty line income increased in real terms between 1979/80 and 1986/87; however, the figures on the distribution of income given in Table 8.5 show a sharp fall in the share of income earned (before transfers and taxes) in the bottom decile. Although the transfer and tax systems did a great deal to ameliorate their position, they were still relatively worse off, in terms of shares in net income, in 1986/87 than in 1979/80. Those below the poverty line in 1986/87 had standardized family incomes (weighted for family size) equal to 43.6 percent of the official poverty line income. This figure compares with 48.1 percent in 1979/80. The earnings system in 1986/87 resulted in a larger number of poor people, whose poverty was relatively greater than in 1979/80. After transfers and taxes are considered, average incomes of the poor came to 77.7 percent of the poverty line income, compared to 77.6 percent in 1979/80.[15]

Conclusion

Between 1984 and 1986 the government reduced its budget deficit mainly by reducing subsidies, freezing certain social expenditures, maintaining very high levels of taxation, and holding down defense spending. This decrease in the deficit helped to reduce inflation in 1985. More fundamental reform has not occurred and the overall level of government intervention in the economy remains high.

Increased expenditure on welfare benefits resulted in pressures on the budget and necessitated high national insurance contributions. It did not, however, prevent an increase in the inequality of income distribution and poverty. The provision of direct services, such as education and welfare, has been squeezed to levels that are almost unacceptably low. In the past few years the need to increase spending on direct services has been recognized (and reinforced by increased immigration) and an attempt has been made to hold back expenditure on social welfare benefits.

Notes

1. L. Meridor, *The Government Budget and Its Relationship to Macro-Economic Developments in Israel 1960–1983* (Jerusalem: Bank of Israel, Discussion Paper Series 86.01, January 1986). In Hebrew.

2. H. Wilkenfeld, *Taxes and People in Israel* (Cambridge, Mass.: Harvard University Press, 1973), p. 16.

3. *Annual Report 1989* (Jerusalem: State Revenue Administration, Ministry of Finance, 1990).

4. *Jerusalem Post Investment Supplement* (Jerusalem: Jerusalem Post, 23 February 1990).

5. *Main Points of the Budget 1991* (Jerusalem: Ministry of Finance, 1990), pp. 51–53. In Hebrew.

6. *Jerusalem Post,* 20 March 1987.

7. G. Ofer, "National Expenditure on Education and Health," in Y. Kop, ed., *Changing Social Policy, Israel 1985–1986* (Jerusalem: Center for Social Policy Studies in Israel, 1986).

8. Ibid.

9. *Quarterly Bulletin* (Jerusalem: National Insurance Institute, 1986/87), vol. 16, no. 2. In Hebrew.

10. *Annual Survey 1987* (Jerusalem: National Insurance Institute, 1988). In Hebrew

11. *Main Points of the Budget 1991* (Jerusalem: Ministry of Finance, 1990), p. 70. In Hebrew.

12. *Annual Survey 1988* (Jerusalem: National Insurance Institute, 1989). In Hebrew.

13. F. Ginor, *Socio-Economic Disparities in Israel* (Tel Aviv: Tel Aviv University, David Horowitz Institute for the Research of Developing Countries, and New Brunswick, N.J.: Transaction Books, 1979).

14. O. Even-Shoshan and Y. Gabbay, "The Distribution of Family Income and Taxes in Israel," in Y. Kop, ed., *Changing Social Policy in Israel 1985–1986* (Jerusalem: Center for Social Policy Studies, 1985).

15. *Annual Survey 1987* (Jerusalem: National Insurance Institute, 1988).

9

Conclusions: The Challenge of Mass Immigration and the Need for Reform

This book has shown how the Israeli economy developed and has analyzed some of the main problems that it encountered in recent years. Its development has been influenced by a number of key factors.

First, Israel is a nation of immigrants: Huge population growth transformed the size of the economy between 1948 and 1970. The increase in the labor force that resulted from immigration brought skills and capital to the country; it also created demand for infrastructure, goods, and services. During the 1970s and 1980s the rate of immigration declined and emigration increased, which resulted in a slower population growth rate and was a factor behind slower economic growth. In 1989 this situation changed: Immigration added 4 percent to the population in 1990.

The second factor was the enormous economic burden of defense. This expense became almost crippling after the 1973 Yom Kippur War and only in recent years has any reduction in defense spending been possible. One consequence of Israel's defense spending was the development of military industries. It led to the successful development of aircraft, electronics, machinery, and other sectors that have had considerable export potential.

In addition to security problems, Israel has been isolated from its neighbors. Its external trade is expensive because of high transport costs, and it has been further hindered by the compliance of many foreign firms with the Arab boycott. Exports have grown and cover a far higher share of the nation's import bill than in the 1950s and 1960s. The growth rate of exports has declined in recent years as has, to an even greater extent, the growth rate of gross domestic product (GDP).

Another burden has been the increased cost of energy. Oil prices rose after 1973 by unprecedented amounts, and in 1975 Israel's oil fields in the Sinai were returned to Egypt. Israel was, therefore, subject to a double squeeze: demand for and the price of oil increased. This situation posed major problems for the balance of payments in the early 1980s.

Domestic economic policy, especially between 1981 and 1984, resulted in accelerated inflation and a worsening balance of payments. This change occurred against the background of higher domestically funded defense costs resulting from the war in Lebanon that started in 1982. By the spring of 1985, the economic crisis had come to a head: Foreign exchange reserves declined to levels that were considered too low, and emergency measures were introduced. As was shown in Chapter 3, this action resulted in a reduction in inflation from 444 percent in 1984 to 185 percent in 1985 and to about 20 percent a year since then.

The source of many of these financial and economic problems has been a series of institutional and political ones. Over twenty-five years ago, it was noted, for example, that the volume of public expenditure was a result of internal social and political pressures rather than of economic priorities. Fiscal policies resulted from compromises between ministries rather than from a unified development plan. The degree of government intervention was justified by the shortage of skilled entrepreneurs and business managers; the government, therefore, had to plan accordingly.[1] For political and ideological reasons, this style of governance suited those in charge of the economy.

Since 1973 Israeli governments have been very weak in dealing with economic problems. The 1974–1977 Labor government managed to reduce the balance-of-payments deficit, against a background of high defense and oil costs. It reformed the income tax system but was unable to restart economic growth. The Labor movement had experienced many divisions and was seriously weakened by the Yom Kippur War. Its ideological legacy was mixed: In the 1960s it shifted policy and put heavy emphasis on private entrepreneurship largely financed by the government. This move was part of a trend toward economic liberalization that, in turn, had its origins in the abolition of rationing, the ending of many import quotas, and the negotiation of an industrial free trade area with the European Community (EC).

The Likud government, which came to power in 1977, was made up of a coalition of liberals who wanted to pursue free market policies and the Herut nationalist party, which favored populist measures. The philosophical split had direct economic consequences: There was a liberalization of the exchange rate system and devaluation but no reduction in public expenditure, which meant that exports could not easily be increased and inflation accelerated. Later, the government, adopting even more populist measures, cut indirect taxes and increased subsidies. The result was an increase in the budget deficit. Little was done to reduce the role of the government in the economy despite the presence of liberals in economic ministries. Rather, the reverse occurred: In order to finance its deficit the government increased the level of its intervention in the economy.

Although industrial management has become more sophisticated and there is a healthier supply of entrepreneurs, it is far from clear that the private sector would provide all the output, investment, employment, and exports needed if the government ended its investment promotion programs and other activities designed to encourage economic development.[2] There is, therefore, a great deal of hesitation about liberalizing the economy, especially in conditions of high unemployment and large-scale immigration.

Between 1984 and early 1990 two coalitions brought the Likud, Labor, and smaller parties to power, thus exasperating conflicts within the government. Decision making continues to be ad hoc and dominated by crises. In the mid-1970s, nearly at the end of the Labor party's long period in office, the situation was described as one in which an informal club of people, who knew each other well, ran the economy. There was centralization of economic decision making whereby the minister of finance could intervene in the affairs of individual firms. At the same time there was an absence of totalitarian or tight bureaucratic control. Control ran informally through a network of personal relationships between top business executives and government leaders. Such a system could not penetrate very deeply into the grass-roots level. Medium- and long-term planning failed: Intentions were not formalized; they were explained on a personal basis to members of the elite. Planning documents were issued but they bore little relationship to reality. The economy and society were, therefore, always in a state of flux.[3] The "club" to a large extent broke down when Labor left office, but as it was not replaced by superior mechanisms, there was actually a deterioration in the quality of economic decision making. A personal connection with a minister can still be as important for a firm as its activity in the marketplace.[4]

This method of operation is typically Israeli: The emphasis is on improvisation; it is very informal and allows each issue to be treated on its merits. The disadvantages are that it lacks consistency and generates continuous uncertainty. This condition is true at all levels: At the senior political level, the cabinet lacks a secretariat to assist in strategy, coordination, or planning. It operates empirically, reacting to crises rather than taking initiatives.[5] Early in 1991 immigration from the Soviet Union slowed down as unemployment in Israel began to affect those who arrived in the country in 1989 and 1990. The government has not been able to put forward comprehensive proposals for solving this problem. The plans that it has come up with were rejected by its own parliamentary supporters as well as by the opposition.[6]

Sources of Division

Political divisions are matched by institutional ones. There is a tendency for the different elites to mistrust one another: The government often views the private sector as primarily interested in tax evasion. The latter regards the state as knowing nothing about business and international competition but as still seeking to control its activities. The Histadrut views the private sector as a competitor that threatens its existence not only through commercial competition but also politically. There are also conflicts of interest, or perceptions of such conflicts, between government departments.

In an address to the Histadrut's founding convention in 1920, one of the leaders of the Labor movement in the Yishuv, Berl Katznelson, made these remarks, still relevant today:

> There are enough men of the right type among the Jewish people but they do not blend into a unified whole. The labor community is burdened on the one hand with work and the upbuilding task, on the other hand with the spiritual and material ruins of Jewry as a whole. Though not yet unified from the organizational point of view it is a living whole in its acts, its essence and its hopes. Though it already stands as an essential part of Jewry, it is torn by internal dissension and strife, out of which no way has yet been found.[7]

The degree of internal conflict in Israeli society is surprising given the degree of external pressure that the country has always been under. In the military field Israel has achieved a unique position internationally, but the lack of cooperation, consensus, and trust in civilian life is sometimes intense. However, there is no precedent for a democracy to be at war for the whole of its independent history: The situation of war and near war is normal for Israelis.

Sectoral Issues

The financial failures of such Histadrut bodies as Koor, Solel Boneh, Alliance, and Kupat Holim in recent years are perhaps most painful because the organization is unique in international terms. Its constituents, such as the kibbutzim, have been admired all over the world as examples of a noncoersive social revolution. Yet, change in human relationships has not been a feature of Histadrut institutions outside the kibbutzim.

The Histadrut's economic enterprises, most of which are connected to Hevrat Ovdim, have never clearly defined their objectives.[8] They have tended to operate for their own benefit rather than for the working class as a whole. The Histadrut has the problem of being both a trade union and an employer: It represents workers in its own factories and other places of work and it owns industries. In the economic sphere it fights for monopolies for its own companies on local markets, while its consumer organization complains about private sector restrictive practices. Added to these issues has been the problem of its image: It is associated in the public mind with the old Labor "aristocracy" that was in power until 1977 and was seen as a closed and increasingly unpopular elite. It has been far from innovative in management-labor relations, which are complex when workers are the owners. Its industrial management has failed to achieve the harmony in industrial relations that exists, for example, in the Spanish Mondragon workers' cooperative.

Managerial attitudes are a problem in sectors other than the Histadrut as well. Private sector attitudes have been conditioned by the fact that the sector owes part of its origins to crucial government decisions in the late 1950s and 1960s. Finance for industry was only available from the state, as was permission for practically everything else that a potential entrepreneur needed. Privately owned companies almost always came to rely heavily on the state: It guaranteed markets by permitting companies to operate local monopolies and protecting them from competitive imports. Maximizing employment and output for the local market was the original aim; companies set up on this basis found it hard to compete internationally. Firms became used to relying on state assistance to such an extent that the government even resorted to buying shares in them when they ran into serious financial problems. This close relationship with the state has hindered the development of a marketing orientation: Some firms that received government assistance have succeeded without having to compete.

The state-owned sector has suffered from a lack of clear direction with regard to its objectives, political interference in its activities, and political appointments to its management and boards of directors. Political appointees do not have to maximize profits or social welfare: They have to remain loyal to the minister who appointed them. After declining in the 1960s the phenomenon of political appointees in the civil service and the public sector has been increasing.

All three sectors operate in an economy that has no mechanism for getting rid of managements that fail. The stock market is dominated by a small number of large operators. Tax regulations are a disincentive with regard to take-overs, which are also regulated by the government. By limiting take-overs, efficiency incentives are also restricted.

Companies have to compete with the state to obtain labor. The public sector increased its labor force and maintained its share of the total, in percentage terms, despite all the pressures to cut public expenditure. It has proved difficult to reduce the labor force in the public sector because many employees have tenured posts and cannot legally be fired. There are also strong political pressures to maintain public sector employment so as to increase the popularity of the minister and political party in charge of the ministry or public sector company. With coalition governments there has been, in effect, competition between politicians to protect their "empires" from spending and employment cuts. Bureaucracy is often blamed for this situation but a more accurate description would be politico-bureaucracy. Politicians have not found it in their interest to reduce administrative impediments; they serve their interests. There is no sufficiently powerful force to overcome these problems and put national interests before sectoral ones.

The Implications for Economic Growth

In the 1970s there was a breakdown in the political and social consensus to put economic growth first. The development of interest groups, which were not willing to put aside their short-term sectoral interests, together with the unfavorable external environment made stagnation inevitable.[9]

The conventional economic debate has always been about the desirability and extent of government intervention in the economy. Intervention was not planned; it was often inconsistent and based on short-term considerations. The relatively small size of the higher civil service group was conducive to "informal" planning.[10] This type of planning meant verbal agreements between sectoral leaders were much more important than explicit, consistent, and feasible planning. The debate has been summarized as being one between those who favored reliance on the price mechanism and those who advocated administrative intervention.[11] The development of a more open economy in the 1960s went hand in hand with an improvement in the balance of payments. In the 1970s and 1980s a more open economy was beneficial in terms of structural change, although other factors limited the growth of the economy.[12]

The Labor government's attitude toward the private sector changed in the 1960s, as it moved away from its socialist ideals and a preference for the Histadrut toward greater reliance on a new class of private entrepreneurs that it financed through the state budget. In the 1970s this relatively new sector reorganized around large banking and Histadrut corporations that exerted considerable influence on the government.[13] As has been shown, the Likud did little to change the basic structure of the economy or to liberalize it.

There is now a wider consensus among economic experts in Israel on the need for reform than ever before. There is also much less naivety about what can actually be done: The pressures under which the government operates are better understood by those who make policy recommendations. There is a consensus that there should be no further nationalization and no abolition of the welfare state.[14]

Government intervention may need to be reduced, but it will remain large because of the problems of defense and the desire to assist in the absorption of immigrants and maintain a welfare state. It is, therefore, necessary to look at the ways in which government intervention can be made more effective as well as the areas where it should be reduced.

The Necessary Reforms

The reforms required to restart economic growth have been outlined in recent years in numerous reports, both official and unofficial. The most important step is the need to reduce the level of fiscal intervention in the economy, which will involve drastically cutting government controls, reducing expenditure, and easing the tax burden. These changes cannot be done without a reduction in defense expenditure, which consumes such a large share of the budget and the national income. Reducing the defense budget will in turn reduce government activity in capital markets, lower the price of capital, and increase its availability to the private sector. A start has been made in opening up financial markets to foreign competition; given the extreme concentration of Israeli banking, more needs to be done.

The government needs to reduce its ownership and control over much of the economy through privatization and decentralization. Appointments to the public service should be professional and not political. Subsidies to capital in industry and for the agricultural use of water should be reduced. A much more vigorous approach will be needed toward the control of those monopolies that survive freer trade. Allocations of credit should be made according to market criteria rather than by central control, as is largely done at present. The wage system needs to be more flexible so as to encourage productivity growth and to enable the economy to attain and maintain international competitiveness, without the regular need for inflationary and disruptive devaluations. Regional policy should be made much more effective by ending capital investment subsidies and increasing expenditure on the infrastructure.

Liberalization of foreign trade is essential: The United States and the EC will not permit free trade agreements to remain in force if they are not mutually beneficial, which means ending the system of hidden import duties. Israel has ended quotas on imports from countries with whom it does not have free trade agreements, but high levels of customs duties will continue to protect various sectors for up to seven years. Antidumping regulations are being strengthened and quotas could be reintroduced. The exchange rate should be unified so as to end the series of hidden taxes and subsidies that a multiple exchange rate mechanism imposes. These are the main reforms needed at the macroeconomic level; there are also numerous changes needed at the sectoral or microeconomic level, which are beyond the scope of this book to detail.

These reforms will prove painful for different groups in the economy. It is, therefore, necessary to be explicit about the kind of politico-economic environment that would most assist in achieving positive results.

The Political Economy of Restarting Economic Growth

The reforms described above have been recommended by economists with different political opinions. The context in which they can best be achieved is seldom examined because political economy is no longer fashionable and because many economists do not feel that it is their province. Yet it cannot be ignored if reform proposals are not to be put forward in a vacuum.

Several types of socio-economic and politico-economic structures have been cited as models for Israel's economic development. The first is the U.S. model of free market capitalism; it is the one to which many Israelis aspire because they know it from personal experience and because they attribute high living standards in the United States to minimal government intervention in the economy. However, in comparison with the United States, Israel has neither scale nor resources. It also lacks an overall free market ideology.

A second model that attracts attention in Israel, as it does elsewhere, is that of the so-called newly industrialized countries of Southeast Asia. Although much can be learned from their experiences there are enormous cultural, social, and political differences that limit the extent to which Israel can replicate conditions there.

Another group of countries provides a possible model that may be much more suitable. At the very least Israelis need to pay more attention to the decision-making systems that these countries use. The smaller countries of Western Europe (Austria, Switzerland, the Netherlands, Scandinavia) and West Germany may be called "corporatist" states. These are mixed economies with public and private sectors in which trade unions, government (of different political complexions), and employers place emphasis on consensus in economic matters. The small European states are liberal market economies; their antiliberalism consists of substituting, where needed, political mechanisms of compromise for the dictates of the market. Conflict is regulated and arbitrated through voluntary, but highly structured, cooperation between the government, unions, and employers. Their economic development has been the result of historical factors. Export specialization linked different economic and social sectors. Urban interests and international economic opportunities weakened the feudal system more than they did in such countries as France and Russia. The importance of foreign trade and the vulnerability of their economies to changes in international markets have been central themes in their development. The business community and trade unions have been integrated into the political decision-making process regarding economic issues. Perhaps the most important feature of their political system is that no group insists on getting all it wants. The need for consensus results in all accepting less than they would like. Hence, consensus has become part of the political and economic culture.[15]

Government action in support of the market has proved successful in Sweden and West Germany, among other countries. Swedish industrial policy, according to the trade unions, has been based on a belief in the efficiency of the market economy. Credit policy was designed to finance efficient compnies and to provide disincentives to the less efficient. The government pursued free trade abroad and restricted monopolies at home. The state does not subsidize the weak.[16]

West German policy has been based on the consensus that modernization should not be hindered by restrictive practices or by government action. Those who lose out from the modernization of an industry or from structural change should be compensated, if necessary by the government. The timing of change is influenced by social considerations, but the process of change is economically determined and, therefore, considered unavoidable.[17] In both Sweden and West Germany the government acts to create a consensus about the need for industrial change. Policies are designed to encourage acceptance of it.

Conditions in Israel are very different. The government has encouraged monopolies, and it has had a restricted interpretation of free trade. Trade unions and employers join together to fight against lower import duties and cheaper imports: They are afraid of the effects of increased competition. They have opposed moves to decentralize and liberalize the economy.[18] The political center of gravity on economic and social issues in these European countries is similar to that in Israel as are their cultural traditions. Most Israelis vote for political parties favoring collectivist policies; both the Likud and Labor are in favor of the welfare state. Liberal parties representing private business interests have only gained seats in the Knesset and ministerial posts in recent years through their connections with the major parties. (The only independent party to campaign for freer markets received about 5 percent of the vote in the 1988 general election.) This collectivist bias transcends deep political differences on other issues in the electorate. Although Israelis complain about the extent of government intervention, they welcome the existence of socially provided services, in part because these form part of the glue that holds the society together. Its institutional structure is similar in some respects to that of the Western European countries described above, but relations between the main political and institutional groups are much more confrontational. The dominant role of defense problems in Israeli life reinforces the tendency toward centralization, but this tendency has not been sufficient, in recent years, to create consensus.

In economic terms the lack of consensus has been most clearly demonstrated in the failure to achieve a real devaluation for more than a short period. This problem became increasingly difficult in the period between 1973 and 1985. The government constantly tried to obtain a real devaluation by reducing the exchange rate, but the indexation of wages and prices resulted in the competitive advantage being wiped out. In July 1985, January 1987, and January 1989 agreements were reached to defer part of the wage compensation due in compensation for price rises. The first package deal represented consensus under the pressure of economic collapse, which was a unique situation rather than the product of a system of consensus-based policy. The second and third devaluations were also made necessary by levels of domestic inflation that had wiped out export competitiveness.

U.S. aid has reduced the incentive to adjust: Israel has had a large cushion for its balance-of-payments deficits in the last fifteen years. This situation has had political and even psychological as well as economic effects. Many organizations, and even individuals, have operated on the basis that someone else would help them balance their books. Usually it was the government that did so, and U.S. aid often made it possible.

Immigration and Israel's Economic Potential

Israel has various advantages that could be used to improve its economic performance. The country has a history of successful adjustment to problems: Between 1948 and 1973 hundreds of thousands of immigrants were absorbed, housed, and trained; they then became part of the society. Wars have been fought and won, development has continued despite the Arab boycott, terrorism, and a degree of international isolation.

A highly educated labor force exists, but there is room for more and better training, particularly of those who do not go on to higher education. The labor participation rate is relatively low, which suggests that there is the potential for increasing the labor force, even without immigration and population growth. The infrastructure exists for increasing labor participation, but more needs to be done to achieve qualitative as well as quantitative change.

The reduction in inflation has gone some way toward improving the business environment, but firms have had difficulties adjusting because of the rapid pace of change. Israelis tend to expect rapid results, but the effects of moving from a period of hyperinflation to one of more normal conditions are not yet fully understood. Lower inflation gives managers more time to deal with problems other than finance.

The current wave of immigration, which includes a large percentage of highly skilled manpower, presents a golden opportunity to fulfill the Zionist dream, strengthen the economy, improve Israel's security, and reduce the per capita defense burden. Potential immigrants in the Soviet Union were, in 1991, delaying their departure to Israel because of rising unemployment there. No small country beset with the problems that Israel faces can easily absorb hundreds of thousands of new immigrants a year. The Israeli government has not implemented policies to absorb new immigrants and to provide them with employment on anything like the scale needed. The absence of a comprehensive and consistent policy is, according to the Bank of Israel, a major factor behind the current rise in unemployment, which could reach 18–19 percent.[19] Immigration would cease and emigration of Israelis would increase.

The proper implementation of government programs would make it possible to absorb the immigrants. It would not be easy, and the population would face restrictions on living standards for some years. Gradually, a larger and more sophisticated economy would emerge.

Israel is unique in having a free trade agreement with the United States and an industrial free trade agreement with the EC. In areas of high value-added production, where transport costs are relatively less significant, these agreements provide an opportunity for foreign investment by Europeans wishing to sell in the U.S. market and vice versa. Israel has, for a small country, a uniquely skilled labor force whose potential has not been fully used.

Notes

1. H. Pack, *Structural Change and Economic Development in Israel* (New Haven: Yale University Press, 1971).
2. *Export Led Growth Strategy for Israel* (Tel Aviv: Jerusalem Institute of Management, 1987).
3. T. Weinshall, "The Industrialization of a Rapidly Developing Country: Israel," in R. Dubin, ed., *Handbook of Work, Organization and Society* (Chicago: Rand McNally, 1976).
4. *Export Led Growth Strategy for Israel.*
5. A. Eban, *An Autobiography* (London: Weidenfeld and Nicholson, 1978).
6. *Ha'aretz* (Tel Aviv), 23 April 1991.
7. Quoted in W. Preuss, *The Labour Market in Israel* (Jerusalem: Rubin Mass, 1965).

8. E. Kleiman, "The Histadrut Economy of Israel: In Search of Criteria," *Jerusalem Quarterly,* no. 41 (Winter 1987).

9. M. Bruno, "Economic Development Problems of Israel," in C. A. Cooper and S. A. Alexander, eds., *Economic Development and Population Growth in the Middle East* (New York: American Elsevier, 1972).

10. N. Halevi and R. Klinov-Malul, *The Economic Development of Israel* (New York: Praeger and Bank of Israel, 1968).

11. M. Michaely, *Foreign Trade Regimes and Economic Development: Israel* (New York: National Bureau for Economic Research, 1975).

12. A. Bregman, *Industry and Industrialization Policy in Israel* (Jerusalem: Bank of Israel, Research Department, 1968). In Hebrew.

13. Introduction to Y. Ben Porat, ed., *The Israeli Economy: Maturing Through Crises* (Cambridge, Mass.: Harvard University Press, 1985).

14. Y. Ben Porat, "The Conservative Turnabout That Never Was," *Jerusalem Quarterly,* no. 29 (Fall 1983).

15. P. Katzenstein, *Small States in World Markets: Industrial Policy in Europe* (Ithaca and London: Cornell University Press, 1985).

16. R. Lawrence and B. Bosworth, "Adjusting to Slower Economic Growth: The External Sector," in B. Bosworth and A. Rivlin, eds., *The Swedish Economy* (Washington, D.C.: Brookings Institution, 1987).

17. J. Esser and W. Fach, "Crisis Management 'Made in Germany': The Steel Industry," in P. Katzenstein, ed., *Industry and Politics in West Germany: Towards the Third Republic* (Ithaca and London: Cornell University Press, 1989).

18. *Ha'aretz,* 1 January 1990. In Hebrew.

19. *Recent Economic Developments* (Jerusalem: Bank of Israel, October 1991), no. 56, p. 1. The governor of the Bank of Israel quoted in *Ha'aretz,* 24 April 1991. In Hebrew.

Bibliography

Books

Arnon, J. *Economy in Turmoil.* Tel Aviv: Hakibbutz Hameuchad, 1985. In Hebrew.

Ben Porath, Y., ed. *The Israeli Economy: Maturing Through Crises.* Cambridge, Mass.: Harvard University Press, 1986.

Bosworth, B., and Rivlin, A., eds. *The Swedish Economy.* Washington, D.C.: The Brookings Institution, 1987.

Cooper, C. A., and Alexander, S. A., eds. *Economic Development and Population Growth in the Middle East.* New York: American Elsevier, 1972.

Eban, A. *An Autobiography.* London: Weidenfeld and Nicholson, 1978.

Gansler, J. *The Defense Industry.* Cambridge, Mass.: MIT Press, 1980.

Gerschenkron, A. *Economic Backwardness in Historical Perspective.* Cambridge, Mass.: Harvard University Press, 1962.

Greenwood, C. S. *Recession as a Policy Instrument: Israel 1965–69.* London: C. Hurst & Co., 1972.

Halevi, N., and Klinov-Malul, R. *The Economic Development of Israel.* New York: Praeger and Bank of Israel, 1968.

Hirsch, S. "Technological Factors in the Composition and Direction of Israel's Industrial Exports." In *The Technological Factor in International Trade,* edited by S. Hirsch. New York: National Bureau for Economic Research, 1970.

Katzenstein, P. *Small States in World Markets: Industrial Policy in Europe.* Ithaca and London: Cornell University Press, 1985.

Katzenstein, P., ed. *Industry and Politics in West Germany: Towards the Third Republic.* Ithaca and London: Cornell University Press, 1989.

Klieman, A. *Israel's Global Reach.* London: Pergamon Brassey's, 1985.

Michaely, M. *Foreign Trade Regimes and Economic Development: Israel.* New York: National Bureau for Economic Research and Columbia University Press, 1975.

Pack, H. *Structural Change and Economic Development in Israel.* New Haven: Yale University Press, 1971.

Patinkin, D. *The Israeli Economy: The First Decade.* Jerusalem: Maurice Falk Institute for Economic Research in Israel, 1967.

Pohoryles, S. *Agriculture in Israel. A Model of Economic Planning.* Tel Aviv: Hakibbutz Hameuchad, 1972. In Hebrew.

Pomfret, R. *Trade Policies and Industrialization in a Small Country: The Case of Israel.* Tubingen: JCB Mohr/Paul Siebert, 1976.

Porter, M. *Competitive Strategy: Techniques for Analyzing Industries and Competitors.* New York: The Free Press, 1980.

Preuss, W. *The Labour Market in Israel.* Jerusalem: Rubin Mass, 1961.

Sarnat, M., ed. *Inflation and Capital Markets*. Cambridge, Mass.: Ballinger, 1978.
Tamari, M. *Some International Comparisons of Industrial Financing*. Stonehouse, Gloucester, England: Technicopy, Ltd., 1977.

Research Papers

1. *Maurice Falk Institute for Economic Research in Israel, Jerusalem*

Barkai, H. *Kibbutz Efficiency and the Incentive Conundrum*. 1987.
Ben Porath, Y. *Patterns and Peculiarities of Economic Growth and Structure*. 1986.
______. *The Entwined Growth of Population and Product 1922–1982*. 1985.
Berglas, E. *Defense and the Economy: The Israeli Experience*. 1983.
Bruno, M. *Israel's Stabilization: The End of the Lost Decade*. 1986.
Halperin, A. *Military Build-up and Economic Growth in Israel*. Falk Institute Conference Paper. Jerusalem. 1986.
Kleiman, E. *Indexation in the Israel Labor Market*. 1985.
______. *The Indexation of Public Sector Debt in Israel*. May 1985.
Klinov-Malul, R. *Israel's Changing Industrial Structure: Years of Growth and Years of Slowdown*. 1984.
Metzer, J. *The Slowdown of Economic Growth in Israel: A Passing Phase or the End of the Big Spurt*. 1986.
Pelzman, J. *The Impact of the US-Israel Free Trade Area Agreement on Israeli Trade and Employment*. 1985.

2. *Israel Center for Social Policy Research, Jerusalem*

Kop, Y., ed. *The Allocation of Resources for Social Services, 1988/89*. In Hebrew.
Weinblatt, G., and Luski, I. *Structure of Salaries in Industry and the Ramifications of Implementing a Minimum Wage*. 1987. In Hebrew.

3. *International Institute for Strategic Studies, London*

Military Balance 1988/89.
Military Balance 1989/90.

4. *Institute for Research of Output and Incomes, Tel Aviv*

Annual Report. 1975, 1981, 1984, 1985, and 1989. In Hebrew.

5. *International Center for Peace in the Middle East, Tel Aviv*

Peri, Y., and Neubach, A. *The Military Industrial Complex in Israel: A Pilot Study*. 1985.

6. Jacob Levinson Center of the Israel-Diaspora Institute, Tel Aviv, and Institute for Jewish Affairs, London

Sussman, Z. *Stagnation, Inflation and the Balance of Payments: Can the Performance of the Israeli Economy Be Improved?* 1985.

7. Jerusalem Institute for Management, Tel Aviv

Export Led Growth: Strategy for Israel. 1987.

8. Stockholm International Peace Research Institute, Stockholm

Yearbook 1983. 1983.
Rivlin, P. "The Burden of Defense: The Case of Israel." In *World Armaments and Disarmament SIPRI Yearbook 1983.* 1983.

Official Sources

All sources are in Hebrew unless otherwise stated.

Bank of Israel, Research Department

Annual Report. 1973, 1974, 1976, 1977, 1981, 1982, 1984, 1985, 1988, 1990.
Recent Economic Developments. September 1985.
Bregman, A. *Industry and Industry Policy in Israel 1965–85.* Research Department Paper, 1986.
Gottleib, D., and Piterman, S. *Inflationary Expectations in Israel.* Research Department Economic Review. 1985.
Liviatan, N., and Piterman, S. *Accelerating Inflation and Balance of Payments Crises: Israel 1973–84.* Research Department Discussion Paper Series, 1984.

Examiner of Banks

Statistics of Israel's Banking System 1984–87.
Annual Survey. 1983, 1984, 1985, 1986.

Bilateral Industrial Research and Development Foundation

Status Report 1986. 1986. In English.

Central Bureau of Statistics

Statistical Abstract of Israel. 1986, 1990.
Monthly Bulletin of Statistics. January 1991.
Tourism and Hotel Service Statistics Quarterly. Vol. 19, no. 3, 1991.

Commission of Enquiry into the Collapse of the Bank Shares

Report, 1986. In Hebrew.

Ministry of Finance

State Budget. 1986, 1990. In Hebrew.
Main Points of the Budget. 1982, 1983, 1984, 1985, 1986, 1988, 1990, 1991.

Government Companies Authority

Accounts of Government Companies, Year to March 1984. 1985.
Accounts of Government Companies, Year to March 1985. 1986.
Accounts of Government Companies, Year to March 1989. 1990.

Ministry of Industry, Supervisor of Restrictive Practices

Patterns of Competition in Israeli Industry. 1984.

Ministry of Science, National Council for Research and Development

Scientific Research in Israel. 1986.

National Insurance Institute

Quarterly Bulletin.
Annual Survey. 1983, 1984, 1987.

Newspapers and Magazines

Davar. Tel Aviv. In Hebrew.
Ha'aretz. Tel Aviv. In Hebrew.
Ma'ariv. Tel Aviv. In Hebrew.
Jerusalem Post. Jerusalem.
The Economist. London.
Industrial Israel. Tel Aviv.

Journals

Columbia Journal of World Business, *New York*

Radom, M. "Military Officers and Business Leaders: An Israeli Study in Contrasts." March/April 1968.

Economic Quarterly, *Tel Aviv (In Hebrew)*

Arnon, J. "Forty Years of the Israeli Economy." Vol. 39, no. 138, November 1988.
Bruno, M. "Economic Stabilization: The Emergency Plan in Its Early Phases." Vol. 37, no. 131, October 1985.
______. "Israel's Crisis and Economic Reform in Historical Perspective." Vol. 40, no. 141, July 1989.
Kleiman, E. "The Cost of Inflation." Vol. 31, no. 120, January 1984.
Kondor, Y. "Capital Utilization, Economies of Scale and Productivity in the Business Sector." Vol. 28, no. 110–111, November 1981.
Lerner, A. "Stabilization and Economic Independence." Vol. 2, no. 5–6, October 1954.

Review of the Federal Board of St. Louis, *St. Louis*

Shiffer, Z. "Money and Inflation in Israel: The Transition of an Economy to High Inflation." Vol. 64, August–September 1982.

The Jerusalem Quarterly, *Jerusalem*

Barkai, H. "Reflections on the Economic Cost of the Lebanon War." No. 37, 1986.
Kleiman, E. "The Histadrut Economy of Israel: In Search of Criteria." No. 41, Winter 1987.

Other Sources

Clal Industries, Ltd. *Annual Report 1985.* Tel Aviv, 1985. In Hebrew.
Hevrat Ovdim. *Economic Report 1985.* Tel Aviv, 1986. In Hebrew.
Neeman, Y., at Conference of the Budget Department of the Ministry of Finance, Jerusalem, January 1987.
Sharon, E., at Conference of the Budget Department of the Ministry of Finance, Jerusalem, January 1987.
Weinshall, T. *Decision Making in Top Management Teams of Israeli Organizations.* Tel Aviv: Tel Aviv University, Faculty of Management Working Paper no. 615/79, July 1979.

International Organizations

International Financial Statistics 1983 Yearbook. Washington, D.C.: International Monetary Fund.
Economic Outlook. Paris: Organization for Economic Cooperation and Development (OECD), December 1984. Historical Series 1969–81, no. 34.

Index